DE QUINCEY, WORDSWORTH AND THE ART OF PROSE

DE QUINCEY, WORDSWORTH AND THE ART OF PROSE

D. D. Devlin

St. Martin's Press   New York

All rights reserved. For information, write:
St. Martin's Press, Inc., 175 Fifth Avenue, New York, NY 10010
Printed in Hong Kong
First published in the United States of America in 1983

ISBN 0–312–19397–1

Library of Congress Cataloging in Publication Data

Devlin, D. D. (David Douglas)
 De Quincey, Wordsworth, and the art of prose.

 Includes bibliographical references and index.
 1. De Quincey, Thomas, 1785–1859—Criticism and
interpretation. 2. Wordsworth, William, 1770–1850—
Criticism and interpretation. 3. Prose literature.
I. Title.
PR4537. D47   1983   828'.809   82–20443
ISBN 0–312–19397–1

To Edith

Of genius, in the fine arts, the only infallible sign is the widening of the sphere of human sensibility. . . . Genius is the application of powers to objects on which they had not before been exercised, or the employment of them in such a manner as to produce effects hitherto unknown.

Wordsworth

Contents

Abbreviation   viii

1 De Quincey and the Magazines   1
2 De Quincey and Wordsworth – I   15
3 De Quincey and Wordsworth – II   48
4 Power and Knowledge   76
5 The Art of Prose   101

Appendix A   122
Appendix B   125
Notes and References   128
Index   131

Abbreviation

Masson   *The Collected Writings of Thomas De Quincey*, ed. David Masson, 14 vols (London, 1896). Roman numerals refer to volumes and arabic numbers to pages.

1 De Quincey and the Magazines

'. . . they won't wait for truth.'

I

In 1805, at the age of 20, De Quincey made a list of the 'Constituents of Human Happiness'. The sixth of these conditions which he needed for a happy life was 'Some great intellectual project, to which all intellectual pursuits may be made tributary'.[1] By 1821, when he was 36 years old, his vague and various ambitious projects had come to nothing, and the need to earn a living had compelled him to begin a career as a writer for magazines with the publication (in its first shorter form) of 'Confessions of an English Opium-Eater' in two successive parts in the *London Magazine* for September and October of that year. For the next thirty years poverty compelled him to publish in periodicals; he saw himself as a hack in an endless struggle with deadlines, and the myth grew of a young romantic (a less unfortunate Chatterton) whose genius was blasted by opium, poverty and the relentlessness of editors, and whose 'great intellectual project' was still-born. 'To win the recognition of editors,' wrote a biographer, 'he needed popular, or semi-popular subjects. Instead of impressive outlay, he must spend his mental wealth in small sums.'[2] Yet in earlier days he had produced nothing. He was widely read in philosophy from Plato to Kant and delighted in scholastic logic, but it is hard to believe that the early ambition to write a comprehensive philosophical work could have come to anything; his mind, as he said, could discover 'by its acuteness not any positive truths', but the errors of other

1

people. It was not health or hardship which thwarted his high ambitions, but temperament. The magazines did not mar the writer: they made him; and De Quincey 'became a man of letters, a figure in English prose, almost in spite of himself'. [3]

For the thirty years after 1821 De Quincey's output was continuous and formidable. There are fourteen volumes in Davis Masson's standard edition of De Quincey's writings, and everything in them except for the short romance called *Klosterheim*, published separately in 1832, had been first published in the pages of one magazine or other. Masson estimates that De Quincey's certain contributions to periodicals between 1821 and his death in 1859 totalled two hundred and fifteen. For the first four years of this thirty-eight year period De Quincy, coming and going between Grasmere and London, wrote almost exclusively for the *London Magazine*. The 'Confessions' had been intended for *Blackwood's Edinburgh Magazine*, but a quarrel with the editor drove De Quincey to London. A letter of introduction from Wordsworth encouraged him to claim help from the editors of the *London Magazine* and the merit of the manuscript which De Quincey produced persuaded them to publish it enthusiastically, without delay and on generous financial terms. De Quincey was usually lucky in his editors; they recognised his merit, paid him well and put up with his endless procrastination and appeals for extension of deadlines. Taylor and Hessey, the editors of the *London Magazine*, lent him money and were so pleased with the profits of the *Confessions* (published as a book in 1822) that they gave him a gift of money, and Blackwood repeatedly lent him money on advance.

By 1825 the London and *London Magazine* connection was over. His own ill-health (the result of his opium addiction), worry over his wife's depression (she stayed behind with her children at Grasmere when De Quincey went to London), shortage of money, inability to write and the cost of travelling to and from London, brought him back to the Lake District. From now on circumstances pointed him in the direction of Edinburgh. His friend John Wilson became Professor of Moral Philosophy in Edinburgh University in 1820 and under the pen-name 'Christopher North' was already becoming one of the most distinguished contributors to *Blackwood's*.

Wilson drew the attention of J. G. Lockhart (now editor of the *Quarterly Review*) to De Quincey and helped to patch up the earlier quarrel with William Blackwood. From now on De Quincey published only in Edinburgh magazines; and for the next twenty-five years, from 1826 to 1850, he worked almost exclusively for *Blackwood's Magazine* and *Tait's Magazine*, but with some important articles in the *North British Review*. By 1849 there was another and unexplained break between De Quincey and *Blackwood's*, and in the same year De Quincey began to contribute to a periodical called *Hogg's Edinburgh Weekly Instructor* (later changed into the monthly *Titan*) which had been started some years earlier by an Edinburgh bookseller, Mr James Hogg. By now, however, De Quincey had reached safer financial waters; and the importance of James Hogg is not that he agreed to publish De Quincey's casual pieces, but that he persuaded him to undertake the task of collecting all his earlier published and unpublished papers into the Edinburgh Edition of his Collected Writings which was at first misleadingly called *Selections Grave and Gay* but finally (and more soberly) *De Quincey's Works*.

II

De Quincey disliked working for magazines; he hated their 'harsh peremptory punctuality' and the need for rapid writing. He complained that some journals had such a strong political bias that they were read only by those who shared the editor's point of view, and that his potential public was thereby much reduced. It was true, he admitted, that every such journal had some circulation 'amongst a neutral class of readers', but although his papers were *printed* in such journals, in many cases they could not be said to have been *published* 'by the ordinary standard of what is understood by publication'. (The italicised distinction is De Quincey's.) 'The papers now presented to the public,' he writes in the 'General Preface' to his Collected Works in 1853, 'like many another set of papers nominally published, were *not* so in any substantial sense.'[4] But his quarrel with journal publication was more than a running resentment that a constant shortage of ready (but not always unready[5]) money drove him into the ambiguous arms

of editors and made him postpone from year to year and
decade to decade that 'great intellectual project' on which his
happiness depended; and it is more than resentment that by
such a mode of publication the number of his readers was
reduced. (In any case, De Quincey admitted that if he lost by
a journal in this way, he also gained by it, since 'the journal
gives you the benefit of its own separate audience, that might
else never have heard your name'.) His objections went much
deeper, and they help to explain his ambitions and intentions
as a prose writer, his belief in the capacities of prose and the
kind of writer he wanted to be.

In the same 'General Preface' De Quincey, among other
complaints, says that writing for the magazines

> . . . drives a man into hurried writing, possibly into saying
> the thing that is not. They won't wait an hour for you in a
> Magazine or a Review; they won't wait for truth; you may
> as well reason with the sea, or a railway train, as in such a
> case with an editor . . . Here is one evil of journal writing –
> viz., its overmastering precipitation. (Masson, I, 6)

This is more than the complaint of someone who disliked
writing against the clock. 'They won't wait for truth.' De
Quincey did not want to think of himself as only a hack writer.
'Like all persons who believe themselves in possession of *original* knowledge not derived from books, I was indisposed to sell
my knowledge for money, and to commence trading author.'
He realised that it was not unprecedented for a writer to sell
what he wrote, but he could not trace any precedent beyond
the early years of the eighteenth century; from which time he
traces in a passage of eccentric literary history what he sees as
the modern corruption of letters.

> First in the eighteenth century all honour to literature,
> under *any* relation, began to give way. And why? Because
> expanding politics, expanding partisanship, and expanding
> journalism, then first called into the field of literature an
> inferior class of labourers. Then first it was that, from the
> noblest of professions, literature became a trade. Literature

it was that gave the first wound to literature; the hack scribbler it was that first degraded the lofty literary artist. For a century and a half we have lived under the shade of this fatal revolution. But, however painful such a state of things may be to the keen sensibilities of men pursuing the finest of vocations – carrying forward as inheritors from past generations the eternal chase after truth, and power, and beauty – still we must hold that the dishonour to literature has issued from internal sources proper to herself, and not from without. (Masson, IV, 312–3)

The 'lofty literary artist' forced to become 'hack scribbler' is a momentary and exaggerated glance at his own position, and De Quincey seems to believe (another romantic notion) that it is neither possible nor desirable to make money while engaged as a writer in the 'eternal chase after truth, and power, and beauty'. But his main complaint is that magazine editors are not interested in any truth or power (a crucial De Quincey critical term to which I shall return) which cannot be easily managed in the small compass or short flight of an article in a journal.

Many eighteenth-century writers, too, wrote in small compass and for money and under 'harsh peremptory punctuality' and also claimed that their aim was truth, though not perhaps power and beauty; and their compass was smaller than De Quincey's and their flights much shorter. De Quincey admired Addison and Johnson; but Addison in *The Spectator* and Johnson in *The Rambler* had to tell the truth in about twelve hundred words, whereas De Quincey's pieces could run to nine thousand words. (Sometimes they could be much longer; his essay on 'Style' came to between thirty and forty thousand words, divided into four parts and published successively in *Blackwood's Magazine* 1840–1.) Truth was not distorted by the tight fit of a *Rambler* essay; 'My other works,' said Dr Johnson, 'are wine and water; but my *Rambler* is pure wine.' Addison in a moment of mischief took as the motto for *Spectator* no. 124 a Greek proverb, 'That a great book is a great evil' and wittily said that his essays offered truth 'in the chymical method, and give the virtue of a full draught in a few drops'.

Were all books reduced, thus to their quintessence, many a bulky author [of, say, some 'great intellectual project'?] would make his appearance in a penny-paper: there would be scarce such a thing in nature as a folio: the works of an age would be contained on a few shelves: not to mention millions of volumes that would be utterly annihilated.

In the same *Spectator* Addison boasted that his papers brought 'knowledge' to the public and 'wisdom' into the streets. Addison and Johnson for several years had to meet dead-lines two or three times a week, and Johnson notoriously found this irksome. For every writer of periodical essays 'the day calls fresh upon him for a new topic, and he is obliged again to choose, without any principles to regulate his choice'. But the writer of essays has this advantage, that 'he seldom harrasses his reason with long trains of consequences . . . or burdens his memory with great accumulations of preparatory knowledge'.[6] In a passage from his valedictory *Rambler* Johnson sums up the problems and pains imposed by what De Quincey calls the 'overmastering precipitation' of writing for the magazines.

He that condemns himself to compose on a stated day, will often bring to his task an attention dissipated, a memory embarrassed, an imagination overwhelmed, a mind distracted with anxieties, a body languishing with disease: he will labour on a barren topic, till it is too late to change it; or, in the ardour of invention, diffuse his thoughts into wild exuberance, which the pressing hour of publication cannot suffer judgment to examine or reduce.

These were the problems: Johnson's merit lay in attempting 'the propagation of truth' for the benefit of those readers only 'whose passions left them leisure for abstracted truth, and whom virtue could please by its naked dignity'. The printer of *The Rambler* and the readers of *The Rambler* did not have to wait for truth: the truth was immediately there. Johnson, like De Quincey, delayed and procrastinated; but when the printer's boy called round for copy and found Johnson not yet risen and the next day's *Rambler* still unwritten, he had only to wait while Johnson dictated 'abstracted truth' from his bed.

It was not, however, this kind of waiting which De Quincey wanted and not this kind of truth which he had in mind. Again and again he contrasted the prose of Johnson and Burke in order to suggest his own different notion of truth and 'the chase after truth'. For Johnson truth did not need to be chased after. It was not to be creatively discovered but was always at hand, and men needed simply to be reminded of it. De Quincey quarrelled with Johnson's conception of truth and therefore with the formal and antithetical prose which conveyed it. He picked on one feature of Burke's conversation and prose (De Quincey does not separate them) which distinguished them from Johnson's:

> It grew; one sentence was the rebound of another; one thought rose upon the suggestion, or more properly upon the impulse, of something which went before. Burke's motion, therefore, was all a going forward. Johnson's, on the other hand, was purely regressive and analytic. That thought which he began with contained, by revolution, the whole of what he afterwards put forth. The two styles of conversation corresponded to the two theories of generation: one (Johnson's) to the theory of *Preformation* (or Evolution), where all the future products, down to the very last, lie secretly wrapped up in the original germ, – consequently nothing is positively added, everything is simply unveiled; the other (Burke's) to the theory of *Epigenesis*, where each stage of the growth becomes a causative impulse to a new stage, – every separate element in the mysterious process of generation being, on this hypothesis, an absolute supervention of new matter, and not a mere uncovering of old, already involved at starting in the primary germ. (Masson, V, 134)

And again, in a phrase that throws light on De Quincey's view of the function of prose, he complains that Johnson never 'GROWS a truth before your eyes'. The 'gyration of his flight upon any one question was . . . exceedingly brief'; there was 'no process, no evolution, no movement of self-conflict or preparation'. Johnson could offer 'a distinction, a pointed antithesis', but there was nothing new in what he said or wrote unless 'a new abstraction of the logic involved in some . . . doubt or prejudice'. Of course he had his uses; 'he unchoked a strangulated sewer in some blind alley'; but, then, 'what river is there that felt his cleansing power'. De Quincey's approving words are of growth and life and new discovery. Conversation need not inhibit the pursuit of truth, but as Platonic dialectic, 'the electric kindling of life between two minds', it could reveal new and subtle truths of a kind more associated with poetry, 'glimpses and shy revelations of affinity, suggestion, relation, analogy'. For Johnson's bare statement of abstracted truth, for a writer who offered you at the end what he already possessed at the beginning (and what, in any case, you already knew), the twelve hundred word gyration of flight was sufficient; and a few sentences of 'automatically antithetic' prose were more than enough to unblock a strangulated sewer. Burke, by contrast, was an original writer; in him 'motion propagated motion and life threw off life'.

> The very violence of a projectile as thrown by *him* caused it to rebound in fresh forms, fresh angles, splintering, coruscating, which gave out thoughts as new (and as startling) to himself as they are to his reader. In this power, which might be illustrated largely from the writings of Burke, is seen something allied to the powers of a prophetic seer, who is compelled oftentimes into seeing things as unexpected by himself as by others. (Masson, X, 270)

Burke had new things to say which could not be said directly, simply and within the restrictions of formally patterned prose. Burke, like De Quincey, is a poet, a seer; but Burke was the lucky one: he did not have to write for the magazines which would not have waited for his kind of truth. A writer like Burke needed time and could get it; but De Quincey complained that he needed time and was denied it. He felt, he said, like the unfortunate author whom he imagined Lord Chesterfield adjuring with the words, 'Come now, cut it short – don't prose – don't hum and haw'. Such an author would not cut it short without dismissing 'the adjuncts that might be necessary to integrate its truth, or the final consequences that might involve some deep *arrière pensée*'. To be brilliant in the rapid fashion demanded by Chesterfield a man can be only 'a refresher of old truths'. He cannot in a short flight be an expounder of new truths, for it will often happen that 'a short and dislocated fraction of the truth is not less dangerous than the false itself'.[7] By new truths De Quincey does not, of course, mean 'truths drawn from fountains of absolute novelty'. The writer is a man speaking to men on the subject of man, and the important truths are those which have long 'slumbered in the mind, although too faint to have extorted attention' and which must be 'awakened into illuminated consciousness'. New truths come from 'gleams of steadier vision that . . . unfold relations else unsuspected'; they come, that is, from imaginative attention. They also come from depth of feeling: 'It is astonishing how large a harvest of new truths could be reaped simply through the accident of a man's feeling, or being made to feel, more *deeply* than other men.'

De Quincey, then, disliked magazine writing because he felt that its limitations (and the need to be immediately understood and popular) allowed no leisure for the 'process', 'evolution', 'movement of self-conflict' and 'long trains of consequence' which are inseparable from the pursuit of truth, or for 'the intricacy and the elaborateness which had been made known to me in the course of considering it'. Magazine articles might do for 'the feebleness of the mere *belle-lettrist*' (and for many readers De Quincey was and is just that) but in such rapidity there can be

> no looking back, so as to adjust the latter sweep of the curve to the former; there can be no looking forward, so as to lay a slow foundation for remote superstructures. There can be no painful evolution of principles; there can be no elaborate analysis; there can be no subtle pursuit of distinction. (Masson, IX, 361)

Only a longer work could provide the complex structure and the awareness of previously unrecognized correspondences and connections that were De Quincey's new truths. A truth of this kind 'is not a piece of furniture to be shifted; it is a seed which must be sown, and pass through the several stages of growth'; it cannot be transferred into a man's understanding from without, but must be made to arise 'by an act of genesis within the understanding'. A new truth is a correction in the human mind's 'mode of seeing', and time must be given for 'the intellect to eddy about a truth and to appropriate its bearings'. To change the reader's 'mode of seeing' and familiarise his mind to a 'complex novelty' the writer must repeat or 'echo' himself by varying the manner of presenting the truth; it must be presented directly and indirectly, at one moment in an abstract shape, at another 'in the concrete'. The 'massy chords' (De Quincey often uses musical imagery and analogies) must be broken 'into running variations'. The language, as always, suggests that 'knowing' the truth is a matter of the growth and movement of the mind.

De Quincey did not claim that writing for the magazines was always restricting or that it always stopped him from telling one kind of truth; it all depended on the kind. Some of his pieces he called 'essays', and the 'essay', as De Quincey defined it, belonged to an inferior genre which addressed itself 'to the understanding as an insulated faculty': that is what made it inferior. An essay states a problem, tries to solve it, and in this attempt it increases our knowledge of the problem. The De Quincey who delighted in formal and scholastic logic found that a magazine article gave space enough for such a limited aim. His essay on 'The Caesars', for example, was not as (he complains) some people thought, 'a simple recapitulation, or *résumé*' of Roman history. He had not given the essays an 'ambitious title' but they had originality; they offered 'indications of neglected difficulty' and sometimes offered solutions of such difficulties; but their originality was of a lesser kind and such 'as ought *not* to have been left open to anybody in the nineteenth century'.[8] But even if we disregard these 'essays' it cannot be said that years of journalism blighted De Quincey's genius or made the wished-for great intellectual project an idle dream. It is difficult to imagine what such a project might have been and impossible to believe it would have been either worth the doing or done well. He mentions two plans from the years 1816–18 which failed to hatch. He tells us in the *Confessions* that he had devoted the labour of his whole life (up to 1821) 'to the slow and elaborate toil of constructing one single work' to which he had given the title of an unfinished work by Spinoza, *De Emendatione Humani Intellectus*. If Spinoza's work remained unfinished, De Quincey's was never begun. Because of 'the Circean spells of opium' and the consequent depression and torpor it lay 'locked up as by a frost'. But when the depression lifted and the opium habit was controlled and the frost thawed, the great work stayed locked up. In 1818 came a second but smaller plan. De Quincey read and was much excited by Ricardo's *Principles of Political Economy and Taxation* (1817); it gave him, he says, a pleasure and an activity which he had not known for years. De Quincey tells us that at this time he was incapable of all general exertion, but with his wife as amanuensis he drew up a 'Prolegomena to all Future Systems of Political Economy'. All this, however, was 'a momentary flash' and 'the "Prolegomena" rested peacefully by the side of its elder and more dignified brother'. It is hard to wish that their rest had been disturbed. Some commentators have seen De Quincey as a failed philosopher. 'He has left us,' one critic complains 'not so much as one essay of original speculation', but was content instead to translate some of Kant's minor or miscellaneous works and to offer 'gossipy accounts' of Kant the man. But De Quincey had something more original to offer than original speculation. Although he was widely read in philosophy ancient and modern he was not a philosopher; a dozen writers were better fitted than he to introduce Kant to English readers, but only De Quincey could turn gossipy accounts into art and find in the magazines a congenial home for 'The Last Days of Emmanual Kant'.

If De Quincey was born (or grew up with) philosophical ambitions, Wordsworth had them thrust upon him by Coleridge; but the instinct or good sense or genius of the two writers led them away (with whatever regrets) from the 'great intellectual projects' of *The Recluse* and the *De Emendatione Humani Intellectus* to a mere *Prelude* to the promised long poem and to articles in magazines, which they both found suitable vehicles, not for 'original speculation', but for what De Quincey found in *Lyrical Ballads*, 'an absolute revelation of untrodden worlds teeming with power and beauty as yet unsuspected among men'.[9] De Quincey learnt (perhaps from Coleridge)

what Coleridge tells us he learnt from his school-master at
Christ's Hospital,

> . . . that poetry, even that of the loftiest and, seemingly, that
> of the wildest odes, had a logic of its own, as severe as that
> of science; and more difficult, because more subtle, more
> complex, and dependent on more and more fugitive
> causes.[10]

For the preparation, logic and revelation of these 'untrodden
worlds' which De Quincey described in the *Confessions, Suspiria
de Profundis,* 'On the Knocking at the Gate in *Macbeth*',
'The Vision of Sudden Death' section in 'The English Mail-
Coach' and a dozen other places, he found the relative shortness of magazine articles entirely suitable; they were the
perfect medium for his equivalent to Wordsworth's 'spots
of time'.

De Quincey admitted that the magazines made him a writer; it was partly that the absolute need to satisfy an editor
conquered what he calls his 'constitutional infirmity of mind'
which 'ran too determinately towards the steep of endless
reverie and of dreamy abstraction from life and its realities'.
But De Quincey was sure not only that the magazines caused
him to write, but that they caused him to write well. It was, he
decided, a very great advantage 'to the eloquent expression of
what a man feels, that he should be driven to express himself
rapidly';

> for when thoughts chase each other as rapidly as words can
> overtake them, each several thought comes to modify that
> which succeeds so intensely as to carry amongst the whole
> series a far more burning logic, a perfect life of cohesion,
> which is liable to be lost or frozen in the slow progress of
> careful composition. (Masson, IX, 360)

The phrases 'burning logic' and 'perfect life of cohesion' are
close to the 'logic' and 'causes' which (in the passage from
Biographia Literaria) Coleridge says he was taught to find in
poetry. But De Quincey is not here thinking of poetry or even
of his own impassioned prose; he has in mind the dozens of

articles (most of them literary–critical) which the magazines forced from him for nearly forty years. Even here the 'inexorable summons' of the weekly or monthly journal unlocked cells in his brain and revealed 'evanescent gleams of original feeling, or startling suggestions of novel truth, that would not have obeyed a less fervent magnetism'.[11] He draws an analogy with personal passion; 'when was it found that a man in passionate anger did or could wander from his theme . . . the essential thoughts could not be otherwise than closely knit.' The magazines might not wait for De Quincey's truth; but *because* they would not wait, they got it.

De Quincey's urgent need to earn a living by publishing piecemeal in the journals was to damage his later reputation as a critic. Because he did not write anything like the 'Preface' to *Lyrical Ballads*, which has a specific, limited aim; or because he did not give to a number of random pieces the spurious unity of being collected and published in one volume, as Coleridge did in *Biographia Literaria*, he has been called 'fragmentary and unreliable'; because his achievement is spread over forty years in the ephemeral pages of a dozen periodicals in London and Edinburgh and is not summed up or graspable in any one place, he is said to lack the 'system, coherence and objectivity of a great critic'.[12]

When De Quincey first appeared in the magazines he was already fully armed as a critic. His earliest essay in criticism (on Richter) was published in *The London Magazine* in 1821 and his essay on *Macbeth* in the same journal two years later when he was 38 years of age. There are no critical juvenilia, no pieces that show us De Quincey moving towards his later critical positions, or discovering a critical method or critical values. For the rest of his life he added nothing to his critical weaponry; he shed no prejudices, modified no enthusiasms, abandoned no earlier positions or former loyalties. There was no preparatory stumbling, for the preparation of the critic had been long, thorough and intense. It began when De Quincey read *Lyrical Ballads* in 1801 and saw this as 'the greatest event in the unfolding of my own mind'.[13] Thereafter it was the profound and constant influence of Wordsworth which (after long gestation) brought the critic De Quincey to birth in 1821. Wordsworth was, in De Quincey's phrase, 'the deep deep magnet' which drew him; and however much Wordsworth the man and De Quincey the opium-eater might later drift apart, the magnet that drew one writer to the other never lost its power, but gave shape, coherence and unity (qualities which De Quincey the critic valued above all others) to what might have remained evanescent gleams and fleeting intuitions. Wordsworth by implication and example gave De Quincey a body of critical theory and value which De Quincey's generalising power and logical skill could shape into a critical position so subtly consistent that it made of forty years of critical essays and articles and notes and digressions a great intellectual achievement to which all his other 'intellectual pursuits were made tributary'.

2 De Quincey and Wordsworth – I

'. . . the deep deep magnet of William Wordsworth.'

I

The magnet drew De Quincey early, and although he probably never saw Wordsworth again after 1829, it never lost its power. De Quincey boasts that he was only fourteen years old when he read his first Wordsworth poem. 'In 1799 I had become acquainted with "We Are Seven"', but, as he told Wordsworth in a letter some years later (1804), he had not come across it in the first edition of *Lyrical Ballads* but in a manuscript copy of the poem which was being circulated in Bath where he was on a holiday visit to his mother. Some time passed before he met Wordsworth's poetry again. As he tells Wordsworth in the same letter in a fuzz of words which makes very little clear, he 'came under the dominion of my passions' (unspecified); 'fell under the influence of the heroes of German Drama' (unspecified); felt himself 'unfettered by any ties of common restraint' (unspecified), and generally indulged in unspecified 'feverish and turbulent dreams of meditation'. Too much specification (even if it had been possible) might have alienated Wordsworth. The point of the letter is to reassure Wordsworth that in spite of all the counter influences he has not lost his love of nature; that he often goes for 'long and lonely rambles through many beautiful scenes'; that in the midst of his malaise he looked round for a guide 'who might assist to develop and to tutor my new feelings' and, remembering the 'deep impression' which 'We Are Seven' had made upon him, knew that in Wordsworth he had found one. De

15

Quincey then read *Lyrical Ballads* extensively (the second 1800 edition) and as a result can reassure a perhaps slightly apprehensive Wordsworth that he now feels 'every principle of good within me purified and uplifted'.[1]

De Quincey was very proud of his early attachment to Wordsworth's poetry and of his early recognition of its genius. He tells in the *Confessions* how in 1802 a cloudscape over the mountains of North Wales reminded him of four lines from Wordsworth's 'Ruth'. 'Was I then, in July 1802, really quoting from Wordsworth? Yes, reader; and I only in all Europe . . . In the winter of 1801–2 I had read the whole of Ruth.'[2] Not quite in the whole of Europe, however. The editor of the *St. James' Chronicle* not only liked the poem but felt that others might like it too, for it was in the pages of that paper that De Quincey (so he tells us) first discovered 'Ruth'. But De Quincey was justly proud; he went to Oxford as an undergraduate in December 1803 and found that his appreciation of Wordsworth was 'in advance of my age by full thirty years'. This admiration was also a profound influence, and he had already made Wordsworth 'operative to my own intellectual culture'. Professor Wilson ('Christopher North') shared the glory with him, and the reader is asked 'to value the prophetic age and intrepidity' of these two acolytes who had 'attached themselves to a banner not yet raised and planted' and were saying about 1802 what 'the rest of the world are saying in chorus about 1832'.[3]

There is some difficulty in dating these early crucial events in De Quincey's mental, emotional and critical history. By 1837 he had moved his early discovery and appreciation of Wordsworth back a little in time. In a chapter of reminiscences he describes a literary society which he attended at Everton, near Liverpool, in 1801. Some of the members wrote poetry; one of the group had at this time just published a translation of a poem from Italian which had 'the moral purpose of persuading young women to suckle their own children'. This was a far cry from Wordsworth, and De Quincey (not surprisingly) was unimpressed. There could be nothing seducing in what they wrote, he said, for they were 'the most timid of imitators'.

But to me, who, in that year, 1801, already knew of a grand

renovation of poetic power – of a new birth in poetry, interesting not so much to England as to the human mind – it
was secretly amusing to contrast the little artificial usages of
their petty traditional knack with the natural forms of a
divine art . . . (Masson, II, 129)

It was in Coleridge as well as Wordsworth that De Quincey
found this 'renovation of poetic power'. In 1801, 'with a beat-
ing heart', he risked reading 'The Ancient Mariner' to Lady
Carbery but did not risk introducing to her any of Wordsworth's poems. The 'new birth in poetry' would have seemed
to her (and to nearly everyone else) abortion; 'and not for the
world would I have sought sympathy from her or from anybody else upon that part of L.B. [*Lyrical Ballads*] which
belonged to Wordsworth.' Not even Coleridge escaped; Lady
Carbery laughed at the finest passages and called the mariner
(though perhaps to tease De Quincey) 'an old quiz'. De Quincey felt that the safest thing to do with Wordsworth's poems
was to 'love and be silent'. He perhaps exaggerated the early
unpopularity of Wordsworth and Coleridge. It seems it was
not simply that in Westmorland 'the neighbouring people, in
every degree' agreed in despising Wordsworth, but the whole
reading public (or rather, the 'one or two in each ten
thousand' who had so much as heard of them) scorned them,
trampled and spat upon them. De Quincey's outrage results
in some confused literary history: they were scorned and spat
upon 'wherever they were known'; but they largely escaped
being scorned and spat upon because they were 'as little
known as Pariahs, and even more obscure'.[4]

De Quincey's young indignation found it hard to stay silent.
Forty years later he recalled, with a mixture of tenderness and
amusement at his early ardent feelings, that it had not been
agreeable to carry 'his devotion about with him, of necessity,
as the profoundest of secrets, like a primitive Catholic
amongst a nation of Pagans', or to feel 'a daily grief, almost a
shame' at nursing a private devotion to what had done more
for 'the expansion and sustenance of my own inner mind' than
'all other literature'.[5] There was no reason, however, why he
should not pour out his veneration and enthusiasm to Wordsworth himself. On the 13th May, 1803, he therefore set
about composing a letter to the poet in which he would

express his 'fervent admiration'. This first attempt, in spite of much revision, failed to satisfy him, and a second was not completed and despatched until 31 May after a final revision and rewriting that kept him busy from nine in the morning until nearly four o'clock in the afternoon. The letter is skilful, fervent and diplomatic. As if by intuition De Quincey guessed (as he wrote later) that Wordsworth was not a man to be openly flattered ('his pride repelled that kind of homage') and that nothing would please him but spontaneous expressions of delight with some passage or poem, or the steady, deliberate praise which came from the 'rational examination, comparison and study of his verse' – practical criticism of a technical, professional kind. De Quincey did not dare (and did not want) to offer the latter, but he could bring 'the homage of an enlightened admirer' and could make it clear that his deep love for Wordsworth's poems was not a 'mere literary preference' but 'went deeper than life or household affections'.[6]

De Quincey had poetic ambitions himself though he was later inclined to deny it; he hinted at these in his letter to Wordsworth but so smothered what he said in double negatives that it is doubtful if Wordsworth would have guessed. Just a day or two before he sent his first letter to Grasmere, De Quincey made a list in his diary of the works which he seriously intended to write. These included verse drama, critical and historical essays, 'a poetic and pathetic ballad', an ode and 'a pathetic poem' which sounds very like a lyrical ballad; it was to describe the emotions of a man dying on a rock in the sea 'within sight of his native cottage and his paternal hills'. He adds that 'I have besides always intended of course that *poems* should form the corner-stones of my fame'. Wordsworth was not the only poet he read. In the diary for April 1803 he makes a list of poets who met his approval. Dryden and Pope are absentees but the list contains no surprises, except for a William Penrose who was later erased. The list includes three modern poets, Southey, Coleridge and, of course, Wordsworth who is given the accolade of three exclamation marks. Chaucer does not appear in the list although De Quincey later claimed in an article published in 1835 that even before 1803 he had read some Chaucer and had felt his 'divine qualities'. One surprise is that there are far more references in the diary to Southey than to Wordsworth.

All other poets (except Coleridge) are ignored in this first letter to Wordsworth. In a reference to *Lyrical Ballads* De Quincey insists that all the pleasure he has received from 'some eight or nine other poets that I have been able to find since the world began – falls infinitely short of what those two enchanting volumes have singly afforded me'. But De Quincey's allegiance to Coleridge would not let him stay silent, and at the end of the letter, having 'bent the knee' before Wordsworth, he adds that 'to no man on earth except yourself and *one* other (a friend of yours) would I thus lowly and suppliantly prostrate myself'. This prostration was not simply to *Lyrical Ballads*. De Quincey refused all his life to separate the writer from his work and did not believe that a bad man could be a good poet. In this first letter he talks of the dignity of Wordsworth's moral character and gives this equal weight with the poet's 'mental excellence' in wishing for his friendship.

There were to be disappointments later; but Wordsworth's answer gave to De Quincey 'a happiness which falls to the lot of few men'. This excellent letter was good-humoured and sympathetic and offered a shrewd wisdom which De Quincey at the time could not have been expected to notice. Wordsworth was pleased that his poems had impressed a stranger 'with such favourable ideas of my character as a man' but he warned that the equation which De Quincey made was perhaps too simple: 'How many things are there in a man's character of which his writings however miscellaneous or voluminous will give no idea.' There was another warning too. To De Quincey's moving and very youthful suing for Wordsworth's friendship came the caution that

> My friendship is not in my power to give: this is a gift which no man can make, it is not in our own power: a sound and healthy friendship is the growth of time and circumstance, it will spring up and thrive like a wildflower when these favour, and when they do not it is in vain to look for it.[7]

To caution was added firm rebuke and critical advice. Wordsworth could not accept De Quincey's total dismissal in his letter of all other poetry; it gave him 'great concern' that De Quincey should place a 'very unreasonable value . . . upon my writings, compared with those of others', and he does not wish to stand in the way 'of proper influence of other writers' and, in particular, of the 'great names of past times'. De Quincey hastened to reply that he had never intended 'to breathe a syllable of disrespect against our elder poets'; he remembered his early list and singled out Milton as the writer who had first waked him to a sense of poetry. Wordsworth was already extending his influence over De Quincey in a valuable way, but something more important was to emerge in the next exchange of letters.

Wordsworth's second letter, written from Grasmere on 6 March 1804, was even more friendly (and much more open) than the first. In it he speaks about his own work; the passage is well known but must be quoted because of De Quincey's response to it. Wordsworth writes that he is now engaged upon 'a Poem on my own earlier life; and have just finished the part in which I speak of my residence at the University'. It would give him, he continues, great pleasure to read this work to De Quincey:

> As I am sure, from the interest you have taken in the L.B. [*Lyrical Ballads*] that it would please you, and might also be of service to you. This Poem will not be published these many years, and never during my lifetime, till I have finished a larger and more important work to which it is tributary. Of this larger work I have written one Book and several scattered fragments: it is a moral and Philosophical Poem: the subject whatever I find most interesting, in Nature Man Society, most adapted to Poetic illustration. To this work I mean to devote the Prime of my life and the chief force of my mind. I have also arranged the plan of a narrative Poem. And if I live to finish these three principal works I shall be content. That on my life, the least important of the three, is better [than] half complete: viz 4 Books amounting to about 2500 lines. They are all to be in blank verse. I have taken the liberty of saying this much of my own concerns to you, not doubting that it would interest you.[8]

In his reply (31 March 1804) De Quincey makes polite and tactful reference to what Wordsworth had called the larger and more important work (*The Recluse*); but

> with a view to my individual gratification, the poem on your
> own life is the one which I should most anxiously wish to
> see finished; and I do indeed look with great expectation for
> the advent of that day, on which I may hear you read it as
> the happiest I shall see.[9]

Even Wordsworth's insistence that the poem on his own earlier life was the least important of his projects could not shake
De Quincey's excited preference for it over the 'moral and
Philosophical Poem' in which, as Coleridge with unwitting
bleakness described, Wordsworth was 'to assume the station
of a man in mental repose, one whose principles were made
up, and so prepared to deliver upon authority a system of
philosophy'. To De Quincey, whose childhood had been so
sad and vivid and shot through by loss, and from which he
would make his finest passages of imaginative reminiscence
and impassioned prose, it must have seemed providential that
'the guide who might assist to develop and tutor' his feelings
had already written on his own days as a child.

In spite of repeated invitations De Quincey did not meet
Wordsworth for three more years, though the magnet had
begun to draw him physically to Grasmere. Twice, it seems, he
travelled to the Lake District and twice turned back. Once he
reached Church Coniston (eight miles from Grasmere) and
once he came so near that he could see the lake and beyond
it Wordsworth's 'little white cottage gleaming from the midst
of trees'. But he dared not go further: 'the very image of
Wordsworth, as I prefigured it to my own planet-struck
eye, crushed my faculties as before Elijah or St. Paul', and he
retreated 'like a guilty thing' to Oxford. The following year,
however (1807), he offered to escort Mrs. Coleridge and her
three young children from Bristol to Keswick. Shortly before
reaching Grasmere De Quincey and the two Coleridge boys
ran ahead of the coach. In a few moments Hartley Coleridge
turned in at a gate and De Quincey knew they he had at last
reached the cottage which was 'tenanted by that man whom,
of all men from the beginning of time, I most fervently desired
to see'. He trembled, but it was impossible to go back, and no

longer conscious of his feelngs he followed Hartley through the gate.

> I heard a step, a voice, and, like a flash of lightning, I saw the figure emerge of a tallish man, who held out his hand, and saluted me with most cordial expressions of welcome. (Masson, II, 230–5)

I do not wish to trace the history of this friendship, its later decay and the gradual estrangement of the two men. Neither was to blame. De Quincey passionately needed more from their friendship than Wordsworth was able (or wanted) to give; and no one could survive unscathed his comparison with Elijah and St. Paul, or the hero-worship and extravagance of 'reverential love' which led De Quincey to vow that he would 'sacrifice even his life' for Wordsworth 'whenever it could have a chance of promoting your happiness'. Many years later De Quincey wrote at length about his slow separation from Wordsworth. 'Men of extraordinary genius and force of mind,' he said in 1840, 'are far better as objects for distant admiration than as daily companions'; it was safer, he felt, 'to scrutinise the works of eminent poets than long to connect yourselves with them', and with wry disillusion he advised his readers not to put their trust in 'intellectual princes'. The words of disappointment stand beside phrases of continuing high regard: for De Quincey Wordsworth always remained a man of extraordinary genius, 'an intellectual prince', 'a grand renovation of poetic power'.[10]

II

De Quincey first heard of *The Prelude* in a letter from Wordsworth in 1804, but could not have read (or have heard Wordsworth read) any part of it before his arrival at Grasmere three years later. It was *Lyrical Ballads* which (he said) had been early 'twisted with [his] heart-strings' and which had led him to seek out Wordsworth; and it was *Lyrical Ballads* which De Quincey all his life found 'scintillating with gems of far profounder truth' than was to be discovered in the 'direct

philosophic poetry' of *The Excursion*. (The heart of De Quincey's objection lies in the adjective 'direct'.) But the Wordsworth influence which shaped De Quincey's progress and
achievement as prose-writer and critic did not come only from
Lyrical Ballads and *The Prelude*: *Lyrical Ballads* also packed a
'Preface'. De Quincey's thinking on criticism took shape not
only from Wordsworth's poetical example but from the critical comments and theories of the 1800 'Preface', the 'Essay,
Supplementary to the Preface' (1815) and from the three
Essays Upon Epitaphs, only the first of which was published in
De Quincey's lifetime, in Coleridge's issue of *The Friend* for 22
February, 1810. (*The Friend* expired before the second and third
essays could be published, but we know that De Quincey had
read them.)

On 21st October 1809 De Quincey moved at last into Dove
Cottage; his association with Wordsworth and with Coleridge
(who was settled at Allan Bank with the Wordsworths and
haphazardly producing *The Friend*) and his physical prox-
imity to them were closer than they would ever be again.
When De Quincey turned author twelve years later he began
to write from a profound knowledge of all Wordsworth's critical prefaces and essays and from deep sympathy with, and
long meditation on Wordsworth's finest poetic work. Tracing
the influence of one writer on another can be an uncertain and
barren business; and in De Quincey's case the tracing can be
confused by the very different presence of Coleridge behind
his thought and writing. I do not wish to show (even if it could
be done) how De Quincey takes aboard this opinion and that
theory, as if they were so much cargo to be moved from one
mind to another. The influence of one great writer is, of
course, not like this and would not be worth attention or comment if it were. From the beginning Wordsworth's influence
was as much moral as literary. Those early, ardent letters tell
us more about De Quincey's 'reverential love' for Wordsworth's moral character than of the 'transcendency' of his
genius; and it is the hope of Wordsworth's friendship, even
more than the poems, that has sustained him through 'two
years of a life not passed in happiness'. It is perhaps more
rewarding to look on Wordsworth not as an influence on De
Quincey, but as an inexhaustible source of energy to him.

De Quincey's poetical ambitions did not long survive his intimacy with Wordsworth and Coleridge. In spite of the implication in his diary for 1803 that '*poems* should form the corner-stones' of his fame, and in spite of the hints in his first letter to Wordsworth that he had 'some spark' of the poet's heavenly fire, he later claimed that he had always doubted whether his 'natural vocation lay towards poetry'. Indeed, De Quincey almost suggests that Wordsworth saved him from a false start; he was a living, awesome definition of what a poet must be, and by providing so high a standard may have saved De Quincey from enlisting 'amongst the *soi-disant* poets of the day' with only their 'skill in appropriating the vague sentiments and old traditionary language of passion'. It is a sign of De Quincey's greatness that his individual talent was not extinguished by the mighty wind of Wordsworth's genius, but burned more brightly because of it. De Quincey's echo of Wordsworth's 1800 'Preface' to *Lyrical Ballads* in his reluctance to discover any essential difference between the language of prose and the language of verse is misleading; we are not listening to his master's voice but to De Quincey's insistence on the equality of prose and verse and to his belief that 'each mode of composition is a great art'. Unlike Wordsworth he will not allow metre to be the distinguishing mark of poetry, for 'distinguishing' might easily become 'distinguished' and could in any case imply a difference. The only opposition is between poetry or impassioned language of any kind and its opposite, 'blank unimpassioned prose'. These, however, are distinctions and definitions to be discussed later. The aim and argument are (like Wordsworth's 'Preface') polemical; De Quincey's ambition is to develop 'the conscious valuation of [prose] style'.

III

De Quincey's first published writing, the anonymous *Confessions of an English Opium-Eater* which appeared in the September and October numbers of the *London Magazine* for 1821, enjoyed an instant success. The publishers were so pleased that they brought it out again in the following year as a book (but still in its original shorter version); and De Quincey and his publishers took further advantage of its popularity by printing in the *London Magazine* in 1823 a number of articles on subjects which might not so easily have tempted the reader (such as 'Anglo–German Dictionaries', 'Prefigurations of Remote Events', 'Moral Effects of Revolutions') had they not been juicily guaranteed to be 'Notes from the Pocket-Book of a late Opium-Eater'. Like 'The Author of Waverley' the ascription of any piece to the 'Opium-Eater' whetted appetites and boosted sales. Nothing else that he wrote except, perhaps, the later frank sketches of Wordsworth, was so successful; but all his life De Quincey was sure of an audience. Editors wanted his work for their magazines, and whatever he wrote they printed. The conditions of magazine writing sometimes oppressed him, but he never had cause to complain of his readers or rely on the dangerous sympathy of devotees. He saw himself often as pariah (a favourite image) or outcast, but was always at ease with his public. He knew that Wordsworth had been less lucky; that 'no applauding coterie ever gathered about him'; and he even exaggerated the poet's unpopularity: 'The neighbouring people, in every degree, "gentle and simple", literary or half-educated, who had heard of Wordsworth, agreed in despising him.' His own happier experience of readers, and his resentment at Wordsworth's hostile early reception, pull him in different directions and keep him from endorsing Wordsworth's angry and contemptuous remarks on the reading public. Indeed, the problem of a writer and his public did not often bother him. He agrees that a poet can never be popular since not one person in a hundred is capable of any 'unaffected sympathy' with poetry; but he does not find refuge from this distressing fact in Wordsworth's desperate distinction between the Public and their 'fallible clamour', and the People whose judgement is infallible (though slow in coming: for Wordsworth the People is almost another name for posterity) and whom 'the Deity inspires'. De Quincey is aware that things have changed since Wordsworth was despised and rejected of men; there is now a much larger reading public or, more accurately, a public capable of reading. This 'new influx of readers' which comes from the growing industrial cities cannot encourage serious literature, for 'to be a reader is no longer, as once it was, to be of a meditative turn'. (It is, he says, 'academic students' alone who keep books alive through the generations.) These new working-class readers have indeed altered the very character of litera-ture. De Quincey could read the signs of the times: a writer of the present day 'to be *very* popular must be a story-teller'.

Wordsworth was angry at his continuing unpopularity but he did not suspect the novel to be a damaging rival; or not until 1842 when he complained that 'Dr Arnold's lads read nothing but Boz'. But De Quincey knew about novels; he even read them. He read Scott, and suspected that Wordsworth hadn't; he read the Brontes; he read Dickens, instalment by instalment, and he read Albert Smith. He liked what he read but he did not approve. (In forty years he only once reviewed a novel.) He saw that 'writers and readers must often act and react for reciprocal degradation'; a barely literate people would demand fiction, and a writer of talent or even genius would have to give it to them.

De Quincey's failure to take the novel seriously has dam-aged his prestige as a critic; and it must seem odd that some-one so intelligently alert to Wordsworth's greatness should be blind to the genius of Dickens or Emily Bronte. It was not that his critical theory and insights could not accommodate fiction, for many excellent scattered comments result very naturally from them; a successful fable, for exampe, is one in which 'the incidents *successively generate each other*'. But from 1799 the over-powering influence of Wordsworth had turned De Quincey towards poetry. Wordsworth, of course, read novels though he largely confined himself to the first half of the eighteenth cen-tury (much to De Quincey's distress he particularly liked Fielding); but in Prefaces, Essays and letters he had nothing to say about fiction. Much of what he said about verse, how-ever, was true, De Quincey saw, of his own imaginative prose; but the novel was something different and lesser. De Quincey saw little in Dickens and spoke with inane condescension of *Wuthering Heights*: 'I fear this lady or gentleman, which ever the author is, is making a mistake. Young ladies, who are the chief readers of novels will never stand to be interested in that sort of people: what they like is some heroic person, say a young or successful officer.' He never mentioned Jane Austen.

He could admire Scott's 'rare art of narrating with brilliancy and effect', but saw nothing more in Thackeray than 'caustic cynicism'. A few earlier novels, *Pilgrim's Progress, Robinson Crusoe, The Vicar of Wakefield,* do rather better. De Quincey's larger objections (and this may seem strange when we think of his later impassioned prose) come from neo-classic theory and reflect those steady and steadying views of literature which lie just below the surface of Wordsworth's critical writings, and which he extended but never abandoned. Wordsworth never tired of praising Sir Joshua Reynolds whose *Discourses* on the principles of art are a handbook of eighteenth-century criticism; but in the Prefaces and Essays we see the neo-classical language beginning to bend under the strain of the enlarged meanings imposed upon it. This bending or (to put it more politely) this wish to reconcile critical opposites appears everywhere in De Quincey's criticism; but he found such reconcilement difficult when discussing fiction, and contented himself with dogmatic, short-sighted dismissal.

The principal objections can be gathered from some comments on the beautiful and the sublime which 'instead of character – that is, discriminating and separating expression, tending to the special and the individual . . . both agree in pursuing the Catholic, the Normal, the Ideal'.[11] The novelist's concern should be with 'the grand central highway of sensibilities of human nature'. 'Extravagance and want of fidelity to nature' (by which De Quincey, like Sir Joshua Reynolds and Dr. Johnson, means general human nature) 'and the possibilities of life are what everywhere mar Dickens to me'. Defoe was a special case: his great achievement was 'circumstantiality'; the endless detail of his books 'makes them so amusing that girls read them for novels' and gives such an air of verisimilitude 'that men read them for histories'. Unfortunately this detail and close texture in Defoe (and even Scott) precludes 'high ideality of mind'.

The novelist, then, 'speaks to what is least permanent in human sensibilities'. He is, of course, to blame for doing this; but this self-degradation is forced on him by the novel form itself and by the nature of the vast number of novel readers. A writer who wishes to be popular must now 'speak through novels', which are 'the one sole class of books' that interest the public or even catch its eye; and the decline in the novel lies in low quality of the new reading public

> [which] must count as a large majority amongst its members those who are poor in capacities of thinking, and are passively resigned to the instinct of immediate pleasure – to them the writer must chiefly humble himself: he must study *their* sympathies, must assume them, must give them back. In our days he must give them back even their own street slang – so servile is the modern novelist's dependence on his *canaille* of an audience. (Masson, IV, 298)

Goldsmith was lucky to have written *The Vicar of Wakefield* (published 1766) before this 'enormous expansion' of the reading public; his sales, no doubt, were smaller, but it was 'a great escape for his intellectual purity'. De Quincey almost reverses Wordsworth's dictum and implies that the public creates the taste which the novelist must satisfy, and which he might even come to enjoy, for every man has 'two-edged tendencies lurking within himself'; one will expand 'the elevating principles of his nature', but the other 'will tempt him to its degradation'. This new audience, literate but uneducated, is now 'strong enough in numbers to impress a new character upon literature'.

> A mob is a dreadful audience for chafing and irritating the latent vulgarisms of the human heart. Exaggeration and caricature, before such a tribunal, become inevitable, and sometimes almost a duty. (Masson, IV, 298–9)

The novelist sinks to the level of his readers; the distinction between genius and hack is lost, and 'the revelations of Albert Smith, Dickens etc. are essentially mean, vulgar, plebeian, not only in an aristocratic sense' (Dickens dealt with the lower classes) 'but also in a philosophical sense'. (This must be one of the most sweeping and depressing etceteras in literary history.)

Fifty years before, in the 'Preface' to *Lyrical Ballads*, Wordsworth had seen these things coming:

For a multitude of causes unknown to former times are now

acting with a combined force to blunt the discriminating powers of the mind and, unfitting it for all voluntary exertion, to reduce it to a state of almost savage torpor. The most effective of these causes are the great national events which are daily taking place and the increasing accumulation of men in cities, where the uniformity of their occupations produces a craving for extraordinary incident . . .

In 1848 De Quincey's complaint is the same; the new factor is the increased popularity of the novel. Novels are all the time becoming 'much more licentious and much grosser', and 'the discriminating powers of the mind' are blunted in those who read them. The novel's great aim is to satisfy the general craving for extraordinary incident; it therefore has to tell a story, and De Quincey (like E. M. Forster) almost wishes that it didn't:

> Finally, the very principle of commanding attention only by the interest of a tale, which means the interest of a momentary curiosity, destined to vanish for ever in a sense of satiation, and the interest of a momentary suspense, that, having once collapsed, can never be rekindled, is in itself a confession of reliance upon the meaner functions of the mind. (Masson, IV, 298)

Even Scott can do little more than perform this mean function well; his greatest gift is 'the rare art of narrating with brilliancy and effect'.

The objection is to a tale that proceeds merely by asking and answering Forster's question, 'And then?'. A more Wordsworthian kind of story is needed. Wordsworth had angrily insisted in the 1800 'Preface' that 'the human mind is capable of excitement without the application of gross and violent stimulants' and that the declared noblest aim of a writer should be to enlarge this capability. De Quincey, too, scorns these stimulants and suggests a different kind of interest:

> How feeble a conception must that man have of the infinity which lurks in a human spirit who can persuade himself that its total capacities of life are exhaustible by the few

gross *acts* incident to social relations or open to human valuation . . . the true internal *acts* of moral man are his
thoughts, his yearnings, his aspirations, his sympathies or
repulsions of heart. (Masson, XI, 80)

He makes an exception of Mrs Radcliffe's novels and other
Gothic romances: but it is not their excitement or narrative
skill that appeals to him: the moving principle of her fiction
is a 'sympathy with the world of conscience' which is heightened 'by association with the shadowy and darker forms
of natural scenery, heaths, mountainous recesses'.[12] Mrs
Radcliffe is recreated in the image of Wordsworth, and De
Quincey's Wordsworthian description of her power could
apply to such passages as the boat-stealing and snare-
robbing episodes in the first book of *The Prelude*.[13]

Other novelists get short shrift. De Quincey could be
prudish: he finds Smollet 'bestial, degrading'; Fielding (whom
Wordsworth read with pleasure) has 'coarse ideals' and
Squire Western is as 'odious' as Tom Jones. Even Richardson
has nothing more to offer the modern reader than 'a gallery of
faded histrionic masquerades'. All of them fail because they
deal of necessity with what is transient, local and particular in
setting and dialogue. To the contemplation of society and
manners novelists apply 'the lower faculties of the mind, –
fancy and the habit of minute distinctions'. In Dr. Johnson's
phrases, they examine the individual, not the species; they
deal with minute discriminations and are too concerned with
the prejudices of their age or country. (De Quincey, like
Wordsworth, maintains but extends neo-classic assumptions.)
Therefore all past novels (even, it seems, Mrs. Radcliffe's)
'have faded almost with the generation that produced them',
and present ones are 'in every language hurrying to decay'.
No single novel-writer will have any long existence, but the
class of such writers, it is true, will always be in demand since
readers look upon novels as mere mirrors and 'seek, in all they
read, to see their own ordinary sentiments reflected'.[14] It is
only 'the grander passions of poetry' that can ally themselves
with forms more abstract and permanent. Poetry for De
Quincey includes impassioned language of any kind; but there

is at least one form of prose fiction which can exhibit the
abstract and the permanent. Like Wordsworth he approves of
the fairy tale, because it can

> restore to man's mind the ideals of justice, of hope, of truth,
> of mercy, of retribution, which else (left to the support of
> daily life in its realities) would languish for want of suffi-
> cient illustration. (Masson, XI, 56)

De Quincey, however, did not share Wordsworth's contempt for novels and their readers, for Boz, 'that Man', and
Dr. Arnold's lads; and common sense led him to find value in
more kinds of fiction than fairy tales. De Quincey (unlike
Wordsworth) was faced with the fact of a vastly increased
reading public and an explosion in the popularity of novels
which were now (he saw) the only books 'that ever interest the
public' or 'reach its heart'. Any writing, even the most popular, that reaches the heart must have some degree of 'power'.
'No man, it may be safely laid down as a general rule, can
obtain a strong hold over the popular mind without more or
less of real power. A reality that must be.' If in any novel a
majority of readers '*feel* a power, and acknowledge a power, in
that case power there must be'. De Quincey finds support in
Dr. Johnson's remark that men do not deceive themselves in
their amusements: 'Asking for *alcohol* he will never be cheated
with water.' This is a great concession, although De Quincey
insists that power is not commensurate with popularity;
power there must be in some degree, but it is the quality of the
power that matters. By this not very clear distinction he seems
to mean that power of a superior kind will be needed to keep a
novel popular with later generations of readers. (De Quincey's
definition of 'power' will be discussed later.) A search of Mrs.
Radcliffe's novels would reveal her 'sympathy with the world
of conscience'. Such glimpses of power can never make novels
important, however. Novels are nearly always engaged with
the 'lower faculties of the mind', but they may at least be
called 'the *minor* key of literature'; only the poets cultivate the
major key. But even this minor key affects us as Wordsworth
claimed that poetry affected us: the 'commonest novel, by
moving in alliance with human fears and hopes, with human

instincts of wrong and right, sustains and quickens those affections. Calling them into action, it rescues them from torpor'; therefore all authors who 'merely *teach*' are lower than 'the meanest that *moves*, or that teaches, if at all, indirectly *by* moving'.

In a chapter of his autobiography De Quincey tells of a coach journey to Lincolnshire at the age of seven. He describes his excitement at the unusually early breakfast, the general bustle and then the sudden sadness before departure in the darkness of a winter morning.

> And many have, doubtless, had my feelings; for I believe few readers will ever forget the beautiful manner in which Mrs. Inchbald has treated such a scene in winding up the first part of her 'Simple Story', and the power with which she has invested it. (Masson, I, 276)

(The word 'power' is always De Quincey's critical Order of Merit; we may take it in the meantime as a rough equivalent of Imagination.) Mrs. Inchbald has here sustained and quickened human hopes and fears; by calling these affections into action she has rescued them from torpor. She has moved her readers and has taught them, if at all, only 'indirectly *by* moving'. The novel, then, can be a branch of the literature of power, although De Quincey seldom finds it to be so in fact. Its power is to make readers 'feel vividly, and with a vital consciousness', emotions which everyday life seldom arouses. The novel must be judged as we would judge poetry; in Goethe's *Wilhelm Meister*, for example, as in his poetry, 'the general current of feeling should be deeper than that of ordinary life'.

Novel readers are therefore wiser than they know. They may go to novels only for amusement, or to see their ordinary sentiments reflected; but they are obeying

> a higher and more philosophic impulse than they are aware of. They seek an imaginary world where the harsh hindrances which in the real one too often fret and disturb the 'course of true love' may be forced to bend to the claims of justice and the pleadings of the heart . . . What they are

striving after, in short, is to realize an ideal, and to repro-
duce the actual world under more harmonious arrange-
ments. This is the secret craving of the reader; and Novels
are shaped to meet it. With what success, is a separate and
independent question. (Masson, XIV, 371)

This separate and independent question is one which De
Quincey scarcely ever tried to answer. Novels might in theory
have power in some degree but he seldom found examples of
it, perhaps because he had no interest in looking for them. He
did not care for novels; and in so far as they had (or might
have) power, he considered them as a feebler kind of poetry
which did not merit or require formal criticism of any kind. If
a novel does have power it will be found in separate passages
(as in the example from Mrs. Inchbald) which will not lose by
being abstracted from the whole. In epic and dramatic poetry
certain rules have acquired an authority 'which may prejudice
the cause of a writer'; but in fiction 'there is no rule which has
obtained any *prescription* . . . but the golden rule of good sense
and just feeling'. A novel seems to be simply a life-like story
with life-like characters. 'How do men generally criticise a
novel? Just as they examine the acts and conduct, moral or
prudential of their neighbours.' They appeal to their own
judgments and their own feelings, for there are not and cannot
be any 'mechanic rules' opposed to 'the natural and spontaneous movements of the unprejudiced judgment'.[15]

Half a dozen comments over thirty years hint that if the
influence of Wordsworth had been less decisive De Quincey
might have moved towards some richer criticism of fiction.
The picaresque tale of Sinbad is condemned because it has
'no unity of interest'. There must be no arbitrary deaths in a
novel, but any character who dies must be disposed of
'agreeably to the providential forecastings of the plot itself,
and by the spontaneous evolution of the fable'. A successful
fable is one in which 'the incidents successively generate
each other'; in the *Iliad* (which De Quincey treats as a
novel) the story 'unfolds like a process of vegetation', and
'the close intertexture' of the several parts 'is as strong a
proof of unity in the design and execution as the intense life
and consistency in the conception of Achilles'. Novels, for

De Quincey, are largely a matter of story and character, but in *Wilhelm Meister* Goethe's treatment of Mignon is condemned because in the movement of the story nothing is 'hastened or retarded by her'; every incident or situation in the novel 'would remain uninjured though Mignon were wholly removed from the story'.

De Quincey condemned novels because they could not offer the catholic, the normal, the ideal, and because he contemptuously considered the 'habit of minute distinction' which they applied to the study of society and manners to be one of the 'lower faculties of the mind'. He had no idea that in his own life-time the novel was becoming (had, indeed, become) the dominant literary form. Neither Wordsworth nor Coleridge had written novels; neither had considered them important; and their own poetic theory and example did nothing to shift De Quincey's gaze from verse to fiction. Yet all his life, but under a different guise, De Quincey delighted in that habit of minute distinction which he rightly saw as the special territory of the novel. In 1839–40 De Quincey wrote a long article in defence of casuistry, and at many other times returned to the same subject. He recognised that there was in England an aversion to the very word because it had been cultivated by the Roman Catholic clergy too much with a view to 'an indulgent and dispensing morality'. This he considers simply an abuse of casuistry; but casuistry proper, 'the application of a moral principle to the *cases* arising in human life', is something we must have, for without it 'no practical decision could be made in the accidents of daily life'. He finds in the people of Great Britain 'a keener sensibility to moral distinctions; more attention to shades of difference in the modes of action; more anxiety as to the grounds of action'.

> In the same proportions among the same people, we may assume a growing and more direct regard to casuistry; which is precisely the part of ethics that will be constantly expanding, and continually throwing up fresh questions. Not as though a moral principle could ever be essentially doubtful; but that the growing complexity of *human* actions will make it more and more difficult in judgment to detach the principle from the circumstances, or, in practice, to

determine the application of the principle to the facts.
(Masson, VIII, 344–5)

The lines might come from an introduction to the Victorian
novel, or from an essay on the genius of George Eliot, who
more than most English novelists takes as her subject the
complexity of human actions and motives, and more than
most is the novelist of casuistry, the moral philosophy of individual cases. George Eliot, indeed, in *The Mill on the Floss*,
offers a similar defence of casuistry in language very close to
De Quincey's:

> The casuists have become a by-word of reproach; but their
> perverted spirit of minute discrimination was the shadow of
> a truth to which eyes and hearts are too often fatally sealed:
> the truth, that moral judgments must remain false and hol-
> low, unless they are checked and enlightened by a perpetual
> reference to the special circumstances that mark the indi-
> vidual lot.

De Quincey finds unprofitable all books written on the model
of Locke's *Essay Concerning Human Understanding*: Locke deals in
general rules and major propositions about which there is no
question, but is silent on how to bring the special case of
conduct under the general rule. Locke deals in aphorisms and
maxims and therefore no one looks to him for guidance in any
moral complexities or dilemmas. All people of strong sense,
George Eliot continues,

> have an instinctive repugnance to the men of maxims:
> because such people early discern that the mysterious com-
> plexity of our life is not to be embraced by maxims . . . And
> the man of maxims is the popular representative of the
> minds that are guided in their moral judgment solely by
> general rules.[16]

For De Quincey casuistry provides 'a special fulness of light'
to those who wish to fulfil their duties; for George Eliot and for
us (but not for De Quincey) the nineteenth-century novel
could provide that light.

In autobiography, too, Wordsworth's example coloured De Quincey's practice; and again De Quincey's reputation has suffered in the twentieth century: his *Confessions* are not considered confessional enough. Virginia Woolf complained that he suffered from 'a tendency to meditative abstraction'; that when he tried to tell the truth about himself 'he shrank from the task with all the horror of a well-bred English gentleman', and that he lacked the candour which led Rousseau to reveal what was ridiculous, mean and sordid in himself. She takes down as evidence and tries to use against him his remark that nothing was more revolting than 'the spectacle of a human being obtruding on our notice his moral vices and scars'; and by judging his autobiographical writings by standards which he would have neither understood nor relished, she fails to see his originality, his indebtedness to Wordsworth and, through him, to eighteenth-century biographical convention.[17]

Virginia Woolf is sure that De Quincey wished to be candid but that he could not lay aside reserve. But candid about what? De Quincey, like Wordsworth and Johnson, saw no interest in moral scars and ulcers. He talks, indeed, of his perfect sincerity; he claims that he has always told 'nothing *but* the truth', but has felt no obligation 'to say the whole truth'; any more than Wordsworth in *The Prelude*, by omitting all reference to Annette Vallon, felt he had compromised the autobiographical truthfulness of his poem.

In *The Rambler*, no. 60, Johnson defines the value of biography (and of autobiography, which he felt more likely to tell the truth):

> I have often thought that there has rarely passed a life of which a judicious and faithful narrative would not be useful. For . . . there is such an uniformity in the state of man . . . that there is scarce any possibility of good or ill, but is common to human kind.

De Quincey's definition shifts the emphasis a little:

> If he were able really to pierce the haze which so often envelops, even to himself, his own secret springs of action and reserve, there cannot be a life moving at all under

intellectual impulses that would not, through that single force of absolute frankness, fall within the reach of a deep, solemn, and sometimes even of a thrilling interest. (Masson, I, 10)

There must be nothing of what Johnson calls 'singularity' in biography or autobiography. De Quincey could have said of his *Confessions* and autobiographical articles what Wordsworth said of *The Prelude*; that it was on 'my earlier life or the growth of my own mind'. And as Wordsworth hoped that his poem would be of 'considerable utility', so De Quincey tells the story of his grief for Kate Wordsworth because he hoped that it might have 'a permanent history in the psychological history of human nature'; and justifies the publication of the *Confessions* in the belief that it will prove 'not merely an interesting record, but, in a considerable degree, useful and instructive'.[18] It would be wrong to suspect cant; though he might extend or expand neo-classic theory he was always unwilling, through temperament and veneration for Wordsworth, to reject it. In addition, De Quincey was a deeply shy man; to use his own phrase, it was not in his power to lay aside reserve. From his birth he 'was made an intellectual creature' and what interested him most was the formation of his mind. He says that into one of his autobiographical articles he had intended to introduce an outline of Kant's transcendental philosophy; not by any logical necessity, 'but as a very allowable digression in the record of [his own] life to whom, in the way of hope and profound disappointment, it had been so memorable an object'.

IV

De Quincey's admiration for *Lyrical Ballads* did not blind him to the confusions and contradictions of the 'Preface' on the subject of poetic diction. Like Coleridge, he was vexed that Wordsworth should have damaged his case by extreme, but equivocal, statements on the language of real life; unlike Coleridge, he saw that Wordsworth's later remarks on language in the *Essays Upon Epitaphs* had (too late, perhaps) corrected and made obsolete and irrelevant his earlier vulnerable position. De Quincey's earliest comments on the 'Preface' are enthusiastic but can be discounted. In 1893 A. H. Japp published for the first time a short essay by De Quincey entitled 'Wordsworth and Southey'.[19] This is obviously, as Japp describes it, an early paper. It is very possible, as one critic has shown, that this is a part of that early defence of the poet which Dorothy Wordsworth had asked him to write in 1809, and which De Quincey claimed to have begun in 1815.[20] It shows the continuing strength of De Quincey's enthusiasm and veneration for Wordsworth in spite of the coolness between them which resulted from De Quincey's marriage with Margaret Simpson. 'Mr. Wordsworth's exposition of his theory is beyond all comparison the subtlest and . . . most finished and masterly specimen of reasoning which has in any age been called forth by any one of the fine arts.' Coleridge's criticisms of it in *Biographia Literaria* (1817) are acknowledged, but for De Quincey 'they fail altogether of overthrowing Mr. Wordsworth's theory'; as for all other critics, they have shown by their 'casual allusions' to the theory that 'they have not yet come to understand what is its drift or main thesis'.

De Quincey's later position was much more critical; he wondered if Wordsworth himself had thoroughly understood his own drift or thesis. Explanation had turned into obfuscation. Coleridge in 1817 was sure that in the 'Preface' lay 'the true origin of the unexampled opposition which Mr. Wordsworth's writings have been since doomed to encounter'; imperfections which might have been forgotten or forgiven 'provoked direct hostility when announced as intentional' and the result of much deliberation.[21] De Quincey came to agree with him. In his essay 'Wordsworth's Poetry' (1845) one original obstacle to the favourable reception of his poetry (and 'an obstacle purely self-created') was his theory of poetic diction. Most readers had paid no attention to the diction until the 'Preface' brought it to their notice. 'Nothing more injudicious was ever done by man.' To make things worse, in the remaining fifty years of his life Wordsworth made no attempt to improve matters, not simply through idleness, 'but also through entire misconception of his own meaning and blind aberration from the road on which he fancied himself moving'.

The novelty of the theory was enough to make Wordsworth unpopular; it made matters worse that the theory was in any case not true. Or rather,

> . . . it was true, and it was *not* true. And it was not true in a
> double way. Stating broadly, and allowing it to be taken for
> his meaning, that the diction of ordinary life (in his own
> words, 'the very language of men') was the proper diction
> for poetry, the writer meant no such thing; for only a *part* of
> this diction, according to his own subsequent restriction,
> was available for such a use. And, secondly, as his own
> subsequent practice showed, even this part was available
> only for peculiar classes of poetry. (Masson, XI, 296)

De Quincey notes that Wordsworth (luckily) did not follow his own advice, and that in 'Laodamia', the sonnets and *The Excursion* 'few are his obligations to the idiomatic language of life, as distinguished from that of books, or of prescriptive usage.'

Wordsworth's 'Preface' may have been injudicious, but De Quincey flirted briefly with one of its theories. Wordsworth was to fit to metrical arrangement 'a selection of the real language of men in a state of vivid sensation'; he had chosen low and rustic life because 'in that condition the essential passions of the heart find a better soil in which they can attain their maturity . . . and speak a plainer and more emphatic language', and because such people 'convey their feelings and notions in simple and unelaborated expressions'. De Quincey, too, was sure that genuine excitement was a guarantee of 'pure idiomatic diction'. 'Real situations are always pledges of a real natural language', but only (it seems) in the letters of 'educated unmarried women above twenty-five'; here is found 'idiomatic propriety, racy in its phraseology, delicate yet sinewy in its composition'. (De Quincey sees no contradiction between propriety and naturalness in language.) Just as equivocal is a comment on Shakespeare who, De Quincey assures us, would (of course) have rejected the company of the gentry for that of 'mechanic and humble tradesmen',Why? Because in such men the feelings are 'more elementary and simple' and thoughts 'speak a plainer language', though

Shakespeare did not take this plainer language as a guide to his own poetic practice. Equivocation disappears in De Quincey's essay 'The English Language'. He there calls it 'a monstrosity' to claim any fine or copious language for an uncultivated people, 'or even for a people of mountaineers' or 'a people in any way sequestered and monotonous in their habits' (Lake District shepherds and dalesmen?). Country people talk about nothing; 'and the fact is, universally, that rural occupations and habits, unless counteracted determinately by intellectual pursuits, tend violently to torpor'.

There is, of course, no equivocation in what De Quincey says about Wordsworth's most notorious assertion in the 'Preface', 'that there neither is nor can be, any essential difference between the language of prose and metrical composition'. Like Coleridge he rejects it and shares the delight which Coleridge expressed at how little 'a mere theory, though of his own workmanship, interferes with the . . . imagination in a man of true poetic genius'. De Quincey could not hesitate in his absolute opposition; partly because the 'great intellectual project' of his life was, perhaps, to establish and validate the art of prose; and partly because he did not judge Wordsworth's poetics from the 'Preface' only, but from his poetry and the later, wiser, non-polemical *Essays Upon Epitaphs*. How could De Quincey accept Wordsworth's assertion that some parts of his best poems would be found 'to be strictly the language of prose, when prose is well written', since his own aim was to show that the language of prose, *especially* when well written, was at a great remove from anybody's best poems?

So, almost for Wordsworth's sake, and in order to undo the damage of the 'Preface', De Quincey makes those counter-assertions which are essential to his own views on prose and which are based on a deeply sympathetic grasp of Wordsworth's genius. The distinction between poetry and prose is profound and is more than a question of diction. (In De Quincey, as in Wordsworth, discussion is sometimes confused because of ambiguity in the word 'language'. Sometimes it is taken to mean 'diction', sometimes 'syntax' and the whole structure of a passage.) Prose is not the negation of verse:

To forbear singing is not, therefore, to speak well or to read well: each of which offices rests upon a separate art of its own. Numerous laws of transition, connexion, preparation, are different for a writer in verse and a writer in prose. Each mode of composition is a great art; well executed, in the highest and most difficult of arts. (Masson, VI, 100)

Even the diction of poetry is everywhere 'a privileged diction'; in serious or impassioned poetry (when poetry is 'well written'?) 'the antique or scriptural language' is everywhere employed; and there are many forms of words which have become with time 'essentially poetic' and cannot be used without either affectation or sentimentality in '*any* mode of prose'. The state of the language co-operated with the religious feeling of the men who translated the Authorised Version of the Bible 'by furnishing a diction more homely, fervent, and pathetic' than would now be available.

Wordsworth at his best uses such homely, antique and fervent language; and it is clear that when he talks of a 'selection of the real language of men in a state of vivid sensation' he includes the real language of men from the previous two centuries. 'Michael' (one of De Quincey's favourite poems) corrects Wordsworth's theory and shows what De Quincey had in mind.

> Of the old man his only son was now
> The dearest object that he knew on earth.
> Exceeding was the love he bare to him,
> His heart and his heart's joy! . . .

> But Isabel was glad when Sunday came
> To stop her in her work: for when she lay
> By Michael's side, she for the two last nights
> Heard him, how he was troubled in his sleep.

>   'Thou must not go:
> We have no other child but thee to lose,
> None to remember – do not go away,
> For if thou leave thy father he will die.'

>   At the sight
> The old man's grief broke from him, to his heart

> He pressed his son, he kissèd him and wept;
> And to the house together they returned.

'Exceeding' as an adjective, 'troubled' with its Biblical echoes, the second person singular 'Thou', 'kissèd' with two syllables, prove De Quincey's point; they could not be used 'in *any* mode of prose' without a sense of 'painful affectation and sentimentality'. By italicising 'any' De Quincey includes in the statement even his own impassioned or poetic prose. Wordsworth's vocabulary is (in this case) simple, but he does not use it simply. De Quincey rejects the words 'simple' or 'simplicity' as a description of Wordsworth's intention or method: the words are too vague and misleading; and he notes again and again that for a 'simple' poet many of Wordsworth's best passages abound in Latinate words. English has a 'double fountain' of words: Saxon and Latin. Each part of the language is good or bad in relation to the subject and the treatment of that subject; and Wordsworth's poems show that this is so.

De Quincey's distinction between the value of the Saxon and Latin elements nearly coincides with the 'two voices' of Wordsworth, and explains that mixture of styles which troubled so many readers, including Coleridge. 'Dictionary words', says De Quincey, (and he means words of Latin or Greek origin) are indispensable to a writer who wishes to excel in 'extent and subtlety of thinking' and in 'elevation and sublimity'; but 'Pathos, in situations which are homely, or at all connected with domestic affections, naturally moves by Saxon words'. ('Do not go away, For if thou leave thy father he will die'.) Lyrical emotion of every kind (which must be in a state of agitation) also needs the Saxon element in English because 'Saxon is the aboriginal element' and therefore 'comprehends all ideas which are natural to the heart of man, and to the *elementary* situations of life'. Polysyllabic words will always be necessary 'in meditative poetry upon solemn philosophic themes'; in that 'meditative pathos' which Coleridge so much admired in Wordsworth. In words which aptly describe much of *The Prelude*, De Quincey says that Latin will predominate in poetry where 'the motion of the feeling is *by* and *through* the ideas' and where the sentiment 'creeps and kindles underneath the very tissues of the thinking'. It is not the case that the true voice of poetry will be heard more clearly in Saxon words:

> It is an error to say that the Saxon part is more advantage-
> ously used for cases of passion . . . Simple narration, and a
> pathos resting upon artless circumstances, – elementary
> feelings, – homely and household affections, – these are
> most suitably managed by the old indigenous Saxon voc-
> abulary. But a passion which rises into grandeur, which is
> complex, elaborate, and interveined with high meditative
> feelings, would languish or absolutely halt without aid from
> the Latin moiety of our language. (Masson, XIV, 157)

It is the principle of Decorum or (as De Quincey more usually calls it) 'appropriateness' which will determine the language of each poem; there can be no prescriptive language, for all things 'have their peculiar beauty and sources of ornament – determined by their ultimate ends, and by the process of the mind in pursuing them'.[22]

De Quincey's clearest description of Wordsworth's views on language is contained in his essay 'Theory of Greek Tragedy' which was published in *Blackwood's* in 1840.[23] He discusses Euripides' innovations in language but makes clear the paral-lel with Wordsworth. The two aims of Greek tragedy (espe-cially of Euripides) and the dangers that threatened their execution were the same as Wordsworth's. These double intentions would be in collision with each other unless most 'artfully managed'. (De Quincey's phrase makes clear that he had no patience with Wordsworth's later abandoned stress on spontaneity.) One aim was to exhibit 'a purified imitation of real human conversation'. There is an echo here of Words-worth's remark that the language of men in low and rustic life was adopted, but 'purified' from its real defects and from all 'lasting and rational causes of dislike or disgust'. Coleridge's famous answer to this was that 'a rustic's language, purified from all provincialism and grossness' (which is what he con-siders causes of dislike or disgust) 'will not differ from the language of any other man of common sense', except that the rustic has fewer notions to convey. De Quincey's statement might seem to be open to the same objection: that a 'purified' imitation of real human conversation will no longer be real human conversation; but the second aim which he notes qualifies the first: it is 'to impress upon this colloquial form, thus far by its very nature recalling ordinary human life, a character of solemnity and religious consecration'. This was achieved in Euripides 'by acts of omission and commission'; what Wordsworth loosely and vaguely called selection, though there was nothing loose or vague in his practice. Wordsworth, too, allowed acts of commission; he had 'of course' in his poems dropped all 'vulgarisms and provincialisms', but he had borrowed sometimes 'a Bible turn of expression'. Euripides banished certain words or forms of words, but he recalled other words 'of high antiquity'. The Greek tragedians including Euripides ('the most Wordsworthian of the Athenian poets') even banished particular tenses, as Wordsworth largely banished the imperfect. This consecration of the tragic style 'was effected by the antique cast, and the exclusive cast, of its phraseology'.

De Quincey was never tempted to blur the distinction between poetry and everyday speech, even its most 'simple and unelaborated expression'. Neither was Wordsworth, except in the 'Preface'; he used the unselected language perhaps only once or twice: the opening line of 'Stepping Westward' and 'He dearly loved their voices' from 'Simon Lee'. Like Euripides, De Quincey knew, and knew that Wordsworth knew, that the language of poetry is everywhere a 'privileged diction'; and he saw that Euripides and Wordsworth had used this privilege to create the 'power of pure (sometimes, we may say, of holy) household pathos'. Indeed, he saw that even in the novel, which was an example (though the lowest) of the literature of power, the language of the dialogue could not be merely the imitation of the real language of men, or even a selection of it; the dialogue 'is meant to be life-like, but still it is a little raised, pointed, coloured, and idealized'.

For the power of this pure pathos De Quincey looks not only to Wordsworth's poetry but to what he says in his *Essays Upon Epitaphs*. In these essays Wordsworth finds that the epitaph is the truest poetry; but in defining that reconcilement of opposites which the epitaph achieves he is defining and describing much of his own finest work. (In an epitaph, writes

Wordsworth in the first *Essay*, 'the passions should be sub-
dued, the emotions controlled; strong indeed, but nothing
ungovernable or wholly involuntary. Seemliness requires this,
and truth requires it also'.) These opposites include, in Coleridge's phrases, 'the general with the concrete', 'the individual with the representative', 'a more than usual state of
emotion with more than usual order'. For De Quincey the
good epitaph is a 'tender expression of household feeling'; its
frank language of natural grief trusts to its own least elaborate
expression or, he adds, 'in the delicacies of covert and circum-
stantial allusion'. An epitaph, that is, unites nature and art,
and De Quincey finds the reconcilement or synthesis
described by Wordsworth in the three *Essays*. He remembers
after twenty-one years (his comments appear in an essay written in 1831) that Wordsworth found the central principle of an
epitaph to lie in its expression of 'the most absolute synthesis
of the generic with the individual':

> that is to say, starting from what a man has *in common* with
> all his species, the most general affections of frail humanity
> – its sufferings and its pleasures, its trials and triumphs, its
> fears and awful hopes . . . it goes forward to what a man has
> most peculiar to himself . . . The first element of an epitaph
> claims the benefit of participation in a catholic interest; the
> second claims it in that peculiar degree which justifies a
> separate and peculiar record. (Masson, V, 102)

De Quincey notes another reconcilement: 'Whatever the
tumultuous agitation or passion' in the mind of the poet or the
writer of an epitaph (like Wordsworth he does not distinguish
between them), yet they have agreed in 'tending to peace and
absolute repose, as the state in which only a sane constitution
of feelings can finally acquiesce'. For De Quincey, as for
Wordsworth, the epitaph is supremely an example of emotion
recollected in tranquillity, of Coleridge's 'more than usual
state of emotion in more than usual order'; or, as Wordsworth
said, 'a conjunction of reason and passion.'

De Quincey refers the reader without qualification to
Wordsworth's three *Essays Upon Epitaphs* because he had
already found in them what he called 'the weightiest thing' he

had ever heard on the subject of language or style; this was
Wordsworth's distinction that words are 'an incarnation of
the thought' and not merely a clothing of it. 'Never in one
word,' writes De Quincey, 'was so profound a truth conveyed', and he eagerly expands it. The truth of it is apparent:

> for, if language were merely a dress, then you could sepa-
> rate the two; you could lay the thoughts on the left hand, the
> language on the right. But, generally speaking, you can no
> more deal thus with poetic thoughts than you can with soul
> and body. The union is too subtle, the intertexture too
> ineffable, – each co-existing not merely *with* the other, but
> each *in* and *through* the other . . . In short, the two elements
> are not united as a body with a separable dress, but as a
> mysterious incarnation. And thus, in what proportion the
> thoughts are subjective, in that same proportion does the
> very essence become identical with the expression, and the
> style become confluent with the matter. (Masson, X, 230)

It is scarcely an exaggeration to say that Wordsworth's
image made De Quincey a critic; he returned to it again and
again: Burke's greatness as a writer lies in his 'incarnating . . .
not dressing his thought in imagery'; imagery is not always
'the mere alien apparelling of a thought' which could be
detached from that thought, 'but is the coefficient that, being
superadded to something else, absolutely *makes* the thought as
a third and separate existence'. Language as incarnation is the
absolute congruence and reconcilement of words and feelings,
if by feelings we understand De Quincey to mean 'forms of
impassioned thought, modes of awareness, felt intuitions'. De
Quincey was reluctant to accept Coleridge's criticism of
Wordsworth's views on language in the 'Preface' to *Lyrical
Ballads* because Coleridge did not see that the notion of language as incarnation in the *Essays Upon Epitaphs* had superseded the earlier criticism, had atoned for the earlier ambi-
valence and had introduced a critical notion of supreme
importance. It is an idea that shapes and gives life to much of
De Quincey's criticism, and to his own theory and practice of
impassioned prose. Wordsworth does not enlarge his brief
image in the third *Essay*, but he follows it with his most

memorable statement of the life and the power for good or evil
that lie in words:

> Language, if it do not uphold, and feed, and leave in quiet,
> like the power of gravitation or the air we breathe, is a
> counter-spirit, unremittingly and noiselessly at work to
> derange, to subvert, to lay waste, to vitiate, and to dissolve.

Language for Wordsworth is a power. For De Quincey language as incarnation leads to power, *is* power; and Wordsworth's insight gives him his central critical idea of the literature of power.

3 De Quincey and Wordsworth – II

'. . . no precedents in any literature.'

I

De Quincey is a disappointing critic of Wordsworth, and his comments on particular poems are few and often thin. It has been calculated that over two hundred allusions to Wordsworth are scattered through his collected works, but they are seldom expanded into comments on Wordsworth's poetic practice or into specific criticisms of his poetry.[1] De Quincey seldom made detailed remarks on the language of any poets (except Milton) and rarely studied poems or even passages from poems. There is praise for Keats's 'Hyperion', but no lines from it are discussed or even quoted; a sympathetic portrait of Shelley contains some quotation but little comment; and in De Quincey's most famous and original critical essay, 'On the Knocking at the Gate in Macbeth', he quotes only one line from the play. Sometimes, indeed, it is possible to wonder how good a critic of poetry De Quincey is, and to throw back at him the accusation he aimed at Wordsworth of a one-sidedness which showed itself in Wordsworth's likings (De Quincey blamed him for praising Cotton extravagantly) but even more in his dislikings; De Quincey was 'appalled' at Wordsworth's contempt for the 'not sufficiently appreciated' verse tales of Harriet Lee.

De Quincey's understanding and criticism of Wordsworth reveals itself indirectly and subtly in comments on his own poetic or impassioned prose, in his evocations and memories of childhood and in his comments on style and what he calls the literature of power; and he writes on these things out of a profound understanding and appreciation of Wordsworth's originality and greatness. This understanding can sometimes be explicit. Nearly all his specific comments are on *Lyrical Ballads* and only a very few are on *The Prelude*. Since the long poem on childhood and the growth of the poet's mind might seem to be closer to De Quincey's ambitions in the *Confessions* and other autobiographical writings, we might have expected him to discuss it or even refer to it more frequently than to the shorter poems. There are reasons for this surprising emphasis but no evidence that De Quincey thought more highly of *Lyrical Ballads* than of *The Prelude*. It is, indeed, a passage from *The Prelude* which receives his highest praise. In an article on Wordsworth published in 1839 De Quincey mentions without (he hopes) any breach of confidence, that 'in a great philosophic poem of Wordsworth's, which is still in MS., and will remain in MS. until after his death, there is, at the opening of one of the books, a dream, which reaches the very *ne plus ultra* of sublimity'.[2] It is, in part, because *The Prelude* is still unpublished that De Quincey seldom discusses extracts from it: 'I scarcely know whether I am entitled to quote . . . any long extract.' Perhaps he overcomes his scruples because the passage from which he quotes twenty lines (the dream passage about the Arab in Book V) was especially interesting and congenial to him; but even here his comment is on the dream and not the language of the dream. It is true that he talks of 'the exquisite skill in the art of composition'; but by composition he means here the form of the dream and not the diction or verse; and, in fact, confessedly quoting from memory 'not refreshed by a sight of the poem for more than twenty years', he remembers the lines inaccurately.

There would be little point in De Quincey's commenting on *The Prelude* in his article on Wordsworth or the Lake Poets, since no reader of the magazines before 1850 could possibly have read it. De Quincey's ambition was to secure recognition and regard for the Wordsworth which was already in print rather than for a Wordsworth poem as yet unknown to the world and which might (and did) remain unknown for many years. The *Lyrical Ballads* had already had some success and not simply a *succès de scandale*; indeed, only a year later (1840)

Wordsworth was able to assure a correspondent that he had received 'testimonies from individuals who live by the labour of their hands, that what I have written has not been a dead letter to them'. Above all, perhaps, he confines his comments largely to *Lyrical Ballads* because these were the first Wordsworth poems he had read and 'the greatest event in the unfolding of my own mind'. The poem to which he most frequently refers is 'We Are Seven' which he had first read in manuscript in 1799, many months before discovering *Lyrical Ballads* from which someone had extracted and copied it. In his first letter to Wordsworth it is *Lyrical Ballads* which he mentions and from which he has the tact to quote; it was *Lyrical Ballads* which determined him to seek the poet's friendship; and it was *Lyrical Ballads* (he said) which completed and established the charm of the Lake District. All his life he talked more about *Lyrical Ballads* than about any other poems of Wordsworth's, perhaps because they brought back to him the happy days of hero-worship when their author was 'to his boyish imagination an ideal tutor and a surrogate for the [school] master he could not respect and the father he did not have'.[3]

Criticism even of *Lyrical Ballads* is scarce, but comment on their originality and greatness is more generous, and shows how De Quincey recognises and endorses Wordsworth's intentions. Coleridge was wrong, says De Quincey, to be persuaded by 'the vulgar superstition in behalf of big books and sounding pretensions' to undervalue Wordsworth's earlier short poems by comparison with his 'direct philosophic poetry'. This is a reference to Coleridge's enthusiasm for *The Excursion*. When De Quincey refers to short poems he is not distinguishing the Lucy poems, say, from 'Michael' or 'The Idiot Boy', but all of them from *The Excursion* and *The Prelude*. The earlier poems, he says, 'are all short'; but though short they are 'generally scintillating with gems of profounder truth' than are to be found in later work. (*The Prelude* as De Quincey knew it was an early poem completed only a few years after *Lyrical Ballads* and as yet unrevised.) When De Quincey defines this profounder truth he repeats with only a slight shift of emphasis what Wordsworth had said in his 'Preface' and what Coleridge had said in *Biographia Literaria*; and at the same time he indirectly describes his own intentions in prose.

I speak of that truth which strengthens into solemnity an impression very feebly acknowledged previously, or truth which suddenly unveils a connexion between objects hitherto regarded as irrelate and independent. . . . Gleams of steadier vision that brighten into certainty appearances else doubtful, or that unfold relations else unsuspected, are not less discoveries of truth than the downright revelations of the telescope . . . It is astonishing how large a harvest of new truths would be reaped simply through the accident of a man's feeling, or being made to feel, more *deeply* than other men . . . The author who wins notice the most is not he that perplexes men by truths drawn from fountains of absolute novelty, – truths as yet unsunned, and from that cause obscure, – but he that awakens into illuminated consciousness ancient lineaments of truth long slumbering in the mind, although too faint to have extorted attention. Wordsworth has brought many a truth into life, both for the eye and for the understanding, which previously had slumbered indistinctly for all men. (Masson, XI, 315)

In his definition of these new truths De Quincey accepts Wordsworth's critical reconcilement of neo-classic and romantic theory. New truths are the discovery of something that was already there (full-grown, ripe and ready to be reaped, in De Quincey's image) which we already knew, and which, as Wordsworth said in the *Essays Upon Epitaphs*, are readmitted by imagination 'into the soul like revelations of the moment'. 'Men,' said Dr. Johnson, 'more frequently require to be reminded than informed'; for Shelley poetry taught us 'to imagine what we know'; 'It is not new light that is to be communicated,' said De Quincey, 'but old torpor that is to be dispersed.' Coleridge had famously noted this when he said that Wordsworth's aim in *Lyrical Ballads* was to direct 'the mind's attention to the loveliness and wonders of the world before us', but which in consequence of 'the film of familiarity' we neither see, hear, feel nor understand.

But Coleridge's description of Wordsworth's aims is inaccurate and insufficient: he confines himself to the external world; but Wordsworth and De Quincey will bring to life truth for both 'the eye and the understanding', and they will do it through steadier vision, through an act of attention. 'I

have at all times endeavoured to look steadily at my subject',
said Wordsworth; and in poem after poem he brings to the
reader's notice these recurring moments of attention: 'I gazed
and gazed' (a phrase repeated in several poems); 'Upon the
moon I fixed my eye'; 'I listened motionless and still'. De
Quincey finds an example of this new 'magical strength of
truth' in a phrase from Wordsworth's 'Address to Kilchurn
Castle' which describes a waterfall seen from some way off as
'frozen by distance'. The effect is perceived at once when
pointed out; but, exclaims De Quincey, 'how few are the eyes
that ever *would* have perceived it for themselves!'. Wordsworth's steadier vision made him look at natural objects
almost more than any other man 'with the eye that neither
will be dazzled from without nor cheated by preconceptions
from within'; he had 'a learned eye'.

Volumes might be filled, says De Quincey, with examples of
this learned eye 'even to the apprehension of the senses', but
Wordsworth looked with equal steadiness of attention at
objects of the understanding. Wordsworth said that he
intended 'to follow the fluxes and refluxes of the mind when
agitated by the great and simple affections of our nature', and
gives as an example 'We Are Seven' in which he aims to show
'the perplexity and obscurity which in childhood attend our
notion of death'. For De Quincey this poem 'brings into day
for the first time' the profound fact that 'the mind of an infant
cannot admit the idea of death, cannot comprehend it'. We
must often have felt 'that there are sorrows which descend far
below the region in which tears gather'; Wordsworth, by an
act of attention of the understanding, wakens this long-
slumbering truth into 'illuminated consciousness' with the
line, 'Thoughts that do often lie too deep for tears'. The writer's task (De Quincey is thinking of himself as well as of
poets) is to offer 'old thoughts surveyed from novel stations
and under various angles'. Wordsworth wins most praise
because he does not perplex men with truths 'drawn from
fountains of absolute originality'; his great distinction, and the
guarantee of his increasing popularity, is the extent of his
sympathy 'with what is *really* permanent in human feelings',
with what Wordsworth called 'the great and universal passions of men', or 'the primary laws of our nature'.

Wordsworth accepts the neo-classic view that writers must deal with normal or general human nature ('We suffer and weep with the same heart; we love and are anxious for one another in the one spirit'[4]) but he greatly extends it. More things are normal or general than we previously thought, and we are encouraged to look for the normal and the general where we might not have expected to find them.[5] De Quincey, indeed, (like Wordsworth) uses Augustan theory to attack the last Augustan, George Crabbe. Wordsworth objected to Crabbe's *The Parish Register* (1807) because it relied too much on facts for its pathos. Telling the facts is not the same as telling the truth, and it is no defence to call this practice true to nature:

> After all, if the Picture were true to nature, what claim would it have to be called Poetry? . . . The sum of all is, that nineteen out of 20 of Crabbe's Pictures are mere matters of fact; with which the Muses have just about as much to do as they have with a collection of medical reports, or of Law cases.[6]

Wordsworth (the year 1808) is now using 'nature' (without a capital) as a synonym for 'mere matters of fact'; and by the conscious reference to 'the Muses' he reminds his correspondent of an earlier and more truthful poetry and poetic theory. James Hogg records a conversation in 1821 when De Quincey attacked Crabbe for similar reasons. Crabbe, he said, was anything but a poet; he did everything to make his subjects flat and commonplace and 'to disrobe them of the garb in which imagination would clothe them, and to bring them down as low as, or even to debase them lower than, the standards of common life. Poetry could no longer exist if cultivated by such writers as Crabbe.'

For De Quincey Wordsworth's aim was entirely different; it was to explore general human nature more thoroughly. He is accused of skimming the surface, 'while in truth he goes very deeply into the elements of our nature, too far indeed for many to follow him'.

> People in general do not sufficiently attend to the principles upon which they act; and Wordsworth's apparent simpli-

city arises in a great degree from his acquaintance with the depths of the human heart and the secret springs that regulate and influence human feelings thoughts and actions.[7]

Many readers object to passages because 'they do not understand the principles on which they themselves act' and accuse Wordsworth of what the eighteenth century called 'singularity', when in fact he is insisting that the proper study of mankind is man and teaching us (in Johnson's words) to 'observe the power of all the passions in all their combinations'. De Quincey, with bizarre consistency, even attacks Wordsworth's tale of 'Margaret' ('The Ruined Cottage'). The dread Jeffrey had praised it; he found 'very considerable pathos in the telling of this simple tale', and he recommended that the tale be cut away from its connection with *The Excursion* (Matthew Arnold later did just that, in an anthology of Wordsworth's verse). Only De Quincey was unsympathetic and wished it to be cut away for another reason. In his attack he employs a Jeffrey-like mixture of mockery and perverse common sense in a facetious re-telling of the story. If the Wanderer had tried 'the effect of a guinea' poor Margaret's decline would have been halted; a brief enquiry at the War Office would soon have placed Margaret 'in communicaton with her truant'. This vapid whimsy continues for several pages before De Quincey reveals more seriously and theoretically his reasons for disliking the tale. The narrative creeps Crabbe-like 'by details and minute touches' instead of 'uttering its pathos through great representative abstractions'.[8]

De Quincey's comments on 'The Ruined Cottage' may seem wilful; but the same consistency seems to lead him to a profound and approving understanding of other characters in Wordsworth's poetry, the famous silent solitaries, such as the old Cumberland beggar, the blind beggar in London, the leech-gatherer, the old soldier, and of those minatory voices of nature that speak with awe and terror to the young boy. De Quincey's comment on Wordsworth is totally indirect and can be gathered only by implication from his own practice in his prose-poems. In a passage from 'Levana and our Ladies of Sorrow' in his *Suspiria de Profundis* he explains these Ladies or Sisters of Sorrow:

These Sisters – by what name shall we call them? If I say simply 'The Sorrows', there will be a chance of mistaking the term; it might be understood of individual sorrow, – separate cases of sorrow, – whereas I want a term expressing the mighty abstractions that incarnate themselves in all individual sufferings of man's heart, and I wish to have these abstractions presented as impersonations, – that is, as clothed with human attributes of life, and with functions pointing to flesh.

And De Quincey goes on to ask,

Do they talk, then? O no! Mighty phantoms like these disdain the infirmities of language. They may utter voices through the organs of man when they dwell in human hearts, but amongst themselves is no voice nor sound ... *Theirs* were the symbols; *mine* are the words. (Masson, XIII, 364–5)

The figures are superior to Wordsworth's Margaret because they are 'abstractions'; they speak for the general human conditions; they deal with what Wordsworth in his *Essays Upon Epitaphs* calls 'the universal intellectual property of man; – sensations which all men have felt and feel in some degree'.[9] In Book VII of *The Prelude* (1805) Wordsworth tells how once in London when he was oppressed by the mystery and the loneliness of 'the overflowing streets',

>   ... 'twas my chance
> Abruptly to be smitten with the view
> Of a blind Beggar, who, with upright face,
> Stood, propped against a wall, upon his chest
> Wearing a written paper, to explain
> The story of the man, and who he was.
> My mind did at this spectacle turn round
> As with the might of waters, and it seemed
> To me that in this label was a type,
> Or emblem, of the utmost that we know,
> Both of ourselves and of the universe;
> And, on the shape of the unmoving man

His fixèd face and sightless eyes, I looked,
As if admonished from another world.
                              (lines 609–22)

The blind beggar is silent and the words on his paper count for
little. He is not a separate case of sorrow but, in De Quincey's
words, is a mighty abstraction that incarnates himself 'in all
individual sufferings of man's heart'. The final line of the
passage also describes the effect of the leech-gatherer on the
poet. He is an abstraction who, because he speaks and moves,
is more clearly 'an impersonation . . . clothed with human
attributes of life, and with functions pointing to flesh'.

What is true of Wordsworth's solitaries is also true of those
things in nature which (in his own words) are 'endowed with
something of the power of life'. In the first Book of *The Prelude*
(1805) he tells that once when he was a boy he took without
permission a shepherd's boat which was moored on the shore
of Ullswater. As he rowed out from the bank

> . . . from behind that craggy steep till then
> The bound of the horizon, a huge cliff,
> As if with voluntary power instinct
> Upreared its head. I struck and struck again,
> And growing still in stature the huge cliff
> Rose up between me and the stars, and still,
> With measured motion, like a living thing,
> Strode after me. With trembling hands I turned,
> And through the silent water stole my way
> Back to the cavern of the willow tree;
> There in her mooring-place I left my bark, –
> And through the meadows homeward went, with grave
> And serious thoughts; and after I had seen
> That spectable, for many days, my brain
> Worked with a dim and undetermined sense
> Of unknown modes of being; in my thoughts
> There was a darkness, call it solitude
> Or blank desertion. No familiar shapes
> Of hourly objects, images of trees,
> Of sea or sky, no colours of green fields;
> But huge and mighty forms, that do not live

Like living men, moved slowly through my mind
By day, and were the trouble of my dreams.

(lines 405–27)

The dark peak stays silent, moves into his mind and heart and
becomes 'an unknown mode of being'. De Quincey's question
and answer about this kind of abstraction are apt. 'Do they talk
then? O no! Mighty phantoms like these' (Wordsworth calls
them 'huge and mighty forms') 'disdain the infirmities of language. They may utter voices through the organs of man when
they dwell in human hearts, but amongst themselves is no voice
nor sound'. De Quincey's remark on the Sisters of Sorrow
shows how early and surely he had grasped the nature and
purposes of Wordsworth's solitaries and of nature made animate. Its very indirection in a context far removed from any
conscious discussion of Wordsworth shows how profoundly
De Quincey was influenced by him, and how deeply sympathetic criticism is to be found by implication in De Quincey's own finest prose.

De Quincey's too rare comments on other shorter poems
show how well he understood Wordsworth. He can comment
on a single word in a stanza from *Peter Bell*:

> Crammed, just as they on earth were crammed;
> Some sipping punch, some sipping tea;
> But, as you by their faces see,
> All silent and all damned.

'How well,' he comments, 'does that one word *silent* describe
these venerable ancestral dinners.' Much more striking is an
insight into the character of a number of poems:

> . . . whosoever looks searchingly into the characteristic
> genius of Wordsworth will see that he does not willingly
> deal with a passion in its direct aspect, or presenting an un-
> modified contour, but in forms more complex and oblique,
> and when passing under the shadow of some secondary
> passion. Joy, for instance, that wells up from constitutional
> sources, joy that is ebullient from youth to age, and cannot
> cease to sparkle, he yet exhibits, in the person of Matthew,

the village schoolmaster, as yet touched and overgloomed by memories of sorrow. (Masson, XI, 301)

From his reading of Wordsworth he finds him to be the poet of paradox, the reconciler of opposites. In 'We Are Seven' 'death and its sunny anti-pole are forced into connexion'; in 'Hart-Leap Well' 'out of suffering there is evoked the image of peace', and from the agony and death of the animal, from the ruined lodge and bowers, from the images of death and dereliction 'the poet calls up a vision of *palingenesis* (or restorative resurrection); he interposes his solemn images of suffering, of decay, and ruin, only as a visionary haze through which gleams transpire of a trembling dawn far off'. This intermingling of the joyous and the sad, 'this reciprocal entanglement of darkness in light, and of light in darkness offers a subject too occult for popular criticism'. Indeed, as he writes elsewhere in remarks that seem to arise from his reading of *Lyrical Ballads*, human nature is so mysterious 'that almost every weighty aspect of truth upon that theme will be found at first sight to be startling, or sometimes paradoxical'. There is no need to hunt for paradox; any man faithful to his own experience will find 'what he *knows* to be the truth' invested by paradox. Let him simply hunt for the truth and 'he will find paradox growing everywhere under his hands as rank as weeds'.

De Quincey notes the same indirectness in *The Prelude*; Wordsworth's growing love of nature as a boy 'by an indirect effect [grew] gradually upon him as he engaged in boyish pursuits'. The poetry reflects this indirection as in the 'there was a boy' passage in Book V where 'the visible scene Would enter unawares into his mind' while the boy listened with intense attention for the owl-calls. From his reading of Wordsworth he notes that 'no mere description, however visual and picturesque, is in any instance poetic *per se*, or except in and through the passion which presides'. In a difficult passage in his *Posthumous Works* De Quincey considers the nature of sin and how the Infinite is made 'operatively familiar' to man, and brings the two ideas dramatically together:

Yes, I affirm that there is no form throughout which the Infinite reveals itself in a sense comprehensible by man and adequate to man; that there is no sublime agency which *compresses* the human mind from infancy so as to mingle with the moments of its growth, positively none but has been in its whole origin – in every part – and exclusively developed out of that tremendous mystery which lurks under the name of sin.

The 'atmosphere of sublimity' that invests every child and the emanations of the infinite which reach it are all 'projections – derivations or counterpositions – from the obscure idea of sin'.[10] Elsewhere he writes that the Greeks and Romans knew about virtue and its antithesis, vice, which was a yielding 'to the seductions of sensual pleasure'. 'But the idea of holiness, and the antithetic idea of sin, as a violation of this awful and un-imaginable sanctity, was ... undeveloped in the Pagan mind.'[11] Such passages can be read as the finest commen-tary we have on 'Nutting' and on several passages in *The Prelude*. 'Nutting' was first published in the second edition of *Lyrical Ballads* and was one of Wordsworth's favourite poems. The boy admires 'the virgin scene' where 'the hazels rose Tall and erect, with milk-white clusters hung'; but for no reason he destroys them:

> Then up I rose,
> And dragged to earth both branch and bough, with crash
> And merciless ravage; and the shady nook
> Of hazels, and the green and mossy bower,
> Deformed and sullied, patiently gave up
> Their quiet being: and, unless I now
> Confound my present feelings with the past,
> Even then, when from the bower I turned away
> Exulting, rich beyond the wealth of kings,
> I felt a sense of pain when I beheld
> The silent trees and the intruding sky.

The boy has yielded to the 'seduction of sensual pleasure' in destroying the beauty of the hazel boughs in this 'virgin scene' or Garden of Eden; but 'the idea of holiness, and the antithetic idea of sin, as a violation of this awful and unimaginable sanctity' are made real in the half animate and minatory presence of the 'silent trees' and the 'intruding sky' which disdain the infirmities of language and strike the mind at the same time with vivid, inseparable intuitions of sublimity and sin.

II

Wordsworth's most frequently remembered remark in the 'Preface' to *Lyrical Ballads*, that poetry was 'the spontaneous overflow of powerful feelings', was also the most misleading. He immediately added that 'Poems to which any value can be attached were never produced on any variety of subjects but by a man who . . . had also thought long and deeply', and never again flirted with the idea of spontaneity or the shallow notion of sincerity that attached to it. All through his life Wordsworth was scornful of any poet wh claimed to write spontaneously and without art; Milton was rebuked for his talk of 'pouring easy his unpremeditated verse', and Wordsworth scorned his own work when it was composed without long and deep thought: 'I stopped at the grave of the poor sufferers and immediately composed the following stanzas; *composed* I have said. I ought rather to have said effused, for it is the mere pouring out of my own feeling.' By 1815 'Multa tulit fecitque, must be the motto of all those who are to last'. But the damage was done; Wordsworth's unforgettable phrase which turned the poet into a Shelleyan skylark borne aloft by currents of hot air, misled even De Quincey. His earlier comments after reading the 'Preface' ecstatically endorsed the notion of spontaneity. On the morning after he had made his first attempt to write a letter to Wordsworth, and perhaps still in a state of excitement, De Quincey noted in his diary that a man of genius

> pours forth his unpremeditated torrents of sublimity – of beauty – of pathos, he knows not – he cares not – how: he is rapt in a fit of enthusiasm or rather in a temporary madness and is not sensible of the workings of his mind any more than the ancient seer – 'wrapt into future times' – during the tide of prophetic frenzy – or a man in the wild delirium of a fever – is conscious of the words he utters. No, Sir: – it is the business of his own accidental coolness or the critic's

perpetual coldness to point out the springs and principles of those 'thoughts that breathe and words that burn' which had spontaneously rushed into his mind.[12]

Contact with Wordsworth tempered this particular overflow of powerful feelings; those long conversations with Wordsworth after De Quincey's arrival at Dove Cottage in November 1804 must have shown him Wordsworth's conviction that the 'rules of art and workmanship ... must be applied to imaginative literature'; that 'the logical faculty has infinitely more to do with poetry than the young and inexperienced, whether writer or critic, ever dreams of', and that the writing of poetry 'requires an adroitness which can proceed from nothing but practice; a discernment, which emotion is so far from bestowing that at first it is ever in the way of it'.[13] Thereafter De Quincey wrote more circumspectly. When he writes in 1834 that 'genius works under a rapture of necessity and spontaneity' he seems to have accepted Wordsworth's distinction between language which is 'artfully' or merely 'artificially' laboured; and the spontaneous overflow of powerful feelings is now opposed, not to art, but to verse which has a 'counterfeit assumption' of passion. De Quincey was never able to shake off the association of spontaneity with sincerity which the 'Preface' had suggested. He was never able to reconcile, as Wordsworth had in the *Essays Upon Epitaphs*, the demands of sincerity and of art; but he would later elevate this failure and avoid the problem by making a critical distinction (to be discussed later) between Eloquence and Rhetoric.

Wordsworth was a narrative poet; about half of the poems in *Lyrical Ballads* tell a story, and in his 'Preface' Wordsworth had important things to say about the kind of story he told and the kind of action he described. The paradoxical title of the collection already gave a hint of his intentions, but Wordsworth made these clear:

... it is proper that I should mention one other circumstance which distinguishes these poems from the popular poetry of the day: it is this, that the feeling therein developed gives importance to the action and situation, and not the action and situation to the feeling.

His stories were to be very different from those told in 'frantic novels' and from the 'deluges of idle and extravagant stories in verse'. De Quincey saw at once the connection between the 'feeling' and the 'story' in these poems as did very few other readers or reviewers. In his *Autobiography* De Quincey promises to tell a story of 'noble revenge'; but in case the word 'revenge' might suggest to the reader something violent and external, he gives a word of caution: 'Yet, perhaps, it is injudicious to have too much excited the reader's expectations; therefore, reader, understand what it is that you are invited to hear – not much of a story, but simply a noble sentiment.' This first caution is followed by a second; the story '(again I warn you) will collapse into nothing at all, unless you yourself are able to dilate it by expansive sympathy with its sentiment'.[14] Wordsworth had made the same point with light seriousness in 'Simon Lee'. The story, or 'incident' as Wordsworth calls it, is a long time telling, but he deftly forestalls the reader's possible impatience with warning words very close to De Quincey's:

> My gentle Reader, I perceive
> How patiently you've waited,
> And now I fear that you expect
> Some tale will be related.
>
> O Reader! had you in your mind
> Such stores as silent thought can bring,
> O gentle Reader! you would find
> A tale in every thing.
> What more I have to say is short,
> And you must kindly take it:
> It is no tale; but, should you think,
> Perhaps a tale you'll make it.

De Quincey adopts the Wordsworthian notion that it is the good reader who makes the good poem; the story is there but requires the co-operation of the reader to make it visible and to make it work. In his *Essay, Supplementary to the Preface* of 1815 Wordsworth says of the pathetic and sublime in poetry that 'without the exertion of a co-operating power in the mind of the Reader, there can be no adequate sympathy with either of those emotions'.

De Quincey is an excellent story-teller. When he is read today it is usually for his evocations of childhood or for the prose-poems in which he recreates and describes his dreams; and the comparison is always with the Wordsworth of *The Prelude*. But scattered through his writings are dozens of tales and anecdotes which in their telling are closer to *Lyrical Ballads*. He praises a book on the history of Greece by saying that its author tells ancient stories not to adorn them, or make clear their moral, but to extract from them 'some new meaning' which would be the illustration 'of some great principle or agency now first revealing its importance'. The 'new meaning', or what Wordsworth called the 'purpose' of the poems in *Lyrical Ballads*, was to emerge when he followed 'the fluxes and refluxes of the mind when agitated by the great and simple affections of our nature'.

De Quincey knew that he was telling his stories in a Wordsworthian way. In 1808 a farmer and his wife, George and Sarah Green, had fallen to their deaths in a snowstorm on their way back to Easedale. They had left six children at home, the eldest an eleven year old girl and the youngest a baby. In the two days before the bodies of their parents were discovered, the eldest girl looked after her young brothers and sisters in their snow-bound cottage and eventually struggled to Grasmere to raise the alarm. When the tragedy was known the Wordsworths organised a fund and the farming-out of the children. Dorothy wrote an account of the disaster, and Wordsworth an unimpressive poem which was published thirty-one years later in *Tait's Magazine*. De Quincey's own memorial was the most moving and the most Wordsworthian. In the same magazine and in the same year (1839) he wrote an account of the incident which he included in an article on 'Early Memorials of Grasmere'. His emphasis was on the bravery and resource of the eldest child. What he has to tell

is not much of a story to excite or impress, unless for those who can find a sufficient interest in the trials and calamities of hard-working peasants, and can reverence the fortitude . . . of a little girl [who] could face an occasion of sudden mysterious abandonment, and could tower up, during one night, into the perfect energies of womanhood. (Masson, XIII, 126)

De Quincey's account is no tale, but if you can bring to it the power of reverence, perhaps a tale you'll make it. Wordsworth's description in the 'Preface' of the 'purpose' of 'The Complaint of a Forsaken Indian Woman' from *Lyrical Ballads* can with only slight exaggeration be applied to De Quincey's story of the Greens: to trace 'the maternal passion' (in De Quincey's case the sisterly passion) 'by accompanying the last struggles of a human being at the approach of death, cleaving in solitude to life and society'.

Many other tales and incidents seem to carry with them an indebtedness to Wordsworth. A slight example can be found in a note which De Quincey added to his enlarged edition of the *Confessions* in 1856. He follows some discussion of 'We Are Seven' with a true story of his own (see Appendix A) to 'impeach the philosophic truth' of that teaching concerning a young child's 'absolute inability' to receive the idea of death which had seemed to De Quincey the purpose of that poem. The story ends in anti-climax; the bird which we expected to recover, dies. The story moves from the actual mispronounced words of the child to her sobbing distress at the death of the bird and to the tears of the narrator; and the tone which was good-humouredly facetious becomes tender and sad; as 'Simon Lee', for example, includes a phrase taken from real life ('dearly loved their voices') and moves from humorous and witty narrative to the tears of the old huntsman and the profounder sadness of the poet. The bird dies at the moment of apparent recovery; as De Quincey said of 'We Are Seven', 'death and its sunny anti-pole are forced into connexion'. The simple fact of the bird's death, coming as and when it does, becomes for the child and the adults (and for us too if we bring to the reading of it a 'power of reverence' or 'thinking heart') a 'vision revealed to all alike' of 'the everlasting mystery of death'. De Quincey said of 'We Are Seven' that it revealed for the first time 'a profound fact in the abysses of human nature . . . that the mind of an infant cannot admit the idea of death'. He tells his story of the bird to dispute 'the philosophic truth' of 'We Are Seven', but this purpose is to reveal another 'profound fact in the abysses of human nature'; that a child of two can see the fact of death with revelatory force.

The story of De Quincey's running away from school is, even in the original shorter version, more subtle in the telling; and partly because it is autobiographical, a memory of childhood, it reminds us of De Quincey's more obvious debt to *The Prelude*. In the later, revised and lengthened version of 1856 the debt and influence are stronger and the mode of telling closer to that of Wordsworth's childhood memories in *The Prelude* than to the more objective telling of *Lyrical Ballads*. There are the complex shifts in time which resemble those of 'The Two April Mornings', many passages of *The Prelude* such as the 'gibbet' passage (Book XI, 1805; Book XII, 1850) (see Appendix B) and Coleridge's 'Frost at Midnight'. The visionary moment, the 'trance, a frost as of some death-like revelation', follows (as with Wordsworth) the moment of acute, profound attention when De Quincey 'gazed with deep emotion at the ancient collegiate church'. Because he knew that it was the last time he would ever see them, he gazed intensely at the various objects in his room; and as in 'The Two April Mornings', intensity of gaze comes from intensity of feeling and later brings intensity of memory.

The most famous part of this passage is the memory within a memory of an earlier visit to the Whispering Gallery of St. Paul's Cathedral which he now sees and describes as an 'involute'. De Quincey's definition of an involute is given in a chapter of autobiography called 'Infant Literature' which begins with a quotation from Wordsworth: 'The child is father of the man'.

> It was, in fact, one of those many important cases which elsewhere I have called *involutes* of human sensibility; combinations in which the materials of future thought or feeling are carried as imperceptibly into the mind as vegetable seeds are carried variously combined through the atmosphere, or by means of rivers, by birds, by winds, by waters, into remote countries. (Masson, I, 128)

This is how De Quincey uses the Whispering Gallery or,

rather, the echo in the gallery. His feeling of 'awe' had been
deepened before he uttered his whisper by the many captured
flags of France and Spain which hung in the cathedral, 'solemn trophies of chance and change amongst mighty nations';
the awe became fear as the whisper of his friend reached him
like a tempestuous uproar and reminded him of the dreadful
irrevocability of all human utterance. Now, two years later,
the 'London menace broke angrily upon me as out of a thick
cloud with redoubled strength'. The gibbet in the passage
which I have mentioned from *The Prelude* is such an involute; as
are in the owl-call passage ('There was a boy . . .' *The Prelude*
Book V, 389–413) the rocks and woods and lake which would
'enter unawares into his mind' (De Quincey says 'carried im-
perceptibly into the mind') and which, variously combined,
are 'materials of future thought and feeling'.

In another chapter of autobiography ('The Affliction of
Childhood') De Quincey makes the matter more clear. There
he tells how on the day after his sister's death he stole up to
her bedroom by the backstairs in order to see her for the last
time:

> But the bed had been moved, and, the back was now turned
> towards myself. Nothing met my eyes but one large win-
> dow, wide-open, through which the sun of midsummer at
> mid-day was showering down torrents of splendour. The
> weather was dry, the sky was cloudless, the blue depths
> seemed to express types of infinity. (Masson, I, 38)

The story of Christ who had suffered death in the sunny cli-
mate of Palestine, and which swayed him 'as mysteriously as
music', now 'slept upon [my] mind like early dawn upon the
waters' and established an early connection between sunshine
and death. He explains why the summer had 'this intense
power of vivifying the spectacle or the thoughts of death':

> And, recollecting it, I am struck with the truth, that far more
> of our deepest thoughts and feelings pass to us through
> perplexed combinations of *concrete* objects, pass to us as *invo-*
> *lutes* (if I may coin that word) in compound experiences
> incapable of being disentangled, than ever reach us *directly*,
> and in their own abstract shapes. (Masson, I, 39)

Such involutes are everywhere in Wordsworth, even in the shortest poems; in 'The Two April Mornings' the cloud with the 'long purple cleft' and the 'slope of corn' are involutes for Matthew, as Matthew himself with his crabstick becomes an involute for the poet. De Quincey's prose-poems, like Wordsworth's poems, have a purpose; but as he says in words which describe the work of both, poetry can speak only 'by deep impulse, by hieroglyphic suggestion. Their teaching is not direct or explicit, but lurking, implicit, masked in deep incarnations'.[15] Such incarnations are involutes.

The influence of *The Prelude* is everywhere in the *Confessions*; in the structure, in the areas of experience explored in both works and in the techniques of exploration. Because for both writers 'thoughts and feelings pass through perplexed combinations of *concrete* objects', or involutes, both works are simultaneously subjective and private in the experiences they record and objective in their technique of presentation. In an essay written in 1845 De Quincey indirectly notes the originality of Wordsworth. He quarrels with a writer on the *Iliad* and *Odyssey* for saying that in them there was 'no sullenness, no querulous complaint, not one personal allusion'. 'But,' asks De Quincey, 'how *could* there have been?' Subjective poetry did not exist in those days:

Not only the powers for introverting the eye upon the *spectator*, as himself the *spectaculum*, were then undeveloped and inconceivable, but the sympathies did not exist to which such an appeal could have addressed itself. (Masson, XI, 386)

By subjective poetry De Quincey means poetry in which the subject is the self. At the time of Homer (and, indeed, even in the Middle Ages where there was the same 'shivering character of starvation as to the inner life of man') 'human feelings and affections were too grossly and imperfectly distinguished'. He quotes with total agreement Wordsworth's comment that when a great writer undertakes such a shift or extension of interest he must 'create the taste by which he is to be enjoyed'; in this case the taste for introverting the eye to inspect the workings of one's own mind. The aim of such inspection is not to look for what is odd or eccentric or unique. De Quincey boldly faces the paradox that threatens to emerge as he contemplates Wordsworth's and his own originality. The great distinction of Wordsworth, for example, and the reason for his increasing popularity, is 'the extent of his sympathy with what is *really* permanent in human feeling'. The problem is, that if an author (like Wordsworth) treats of 'what lies deepest in man' he will encounter the greatest 'strength of resistance in the public taste'. In this discovery of what lies deepest, of new areas of our common humanity, lies the true originality of the writer; whatever (in this sense) is 'too original will be hated at the first. It must slowly mould a public'.[16] In his autobiography De Quincey tells of his intense grief at the death of Wordsworth's three year old daughter Catherine. On hearing the news he hastily returned to Grasmere and 'stretched myself every night, for more than two months running upon her grave'. He tells us of this extreme behaviour, not because it is 'a psychological curiosity – a hollow thing', but because it has 'a permanent interest in the psychological history of human nature'. Indeed, to make the point more firmly, he insists that 'all experienced physicians know well that cases similar to mine, though not common, occur at intervals in every large community'.[17] In the original version De Quincey made clear his wish to raise the *Confessions* above the level of gossip, to disown, indeed, the confessional implications of the title. It is not enough that the reader should find the work interesting: he must also find it useful and instructive. He claims (a little mockingly) to write as a philosopher, as one, that is, who must possess not only 'a superb intellect in its analytic functions' but also 'an inner eye and power of intuition for the vision and the mysteries of our human nature'. We do not need the quotation from 'I wandered lonely as a cloud' ('inner eye') to make us feel that he is thinking of Wordsworth, for he goes on to attribute this quality in the highest degree to the English poets. De Quincey will use these twin capacities on himself, on the *spectator* as *spectaculum*, to widen our vision of what human nature is.

De Quincey's involutes or incarnations shape the adult consciousness which will ever after recall, and in recalling reinforce, those early experiences or sensations which were born through concrete objects. Like Wordsworth's 'spots of time' these involutes occur most frequently in childhood.

> There are in our existence spots of time,
> Which with distinct pre-eminence retain
> A vivifying virtue, whence . . . our minds
> Are nourished and invisibly repaired . . .
> Such moments, worthy of all gratitude,
> Are scattered everywhere, taking their date
> From our first childhood: in our childhood even
> Perhaps are most conspicuous.
>   (*The Prelude* (1805) Book XI, 258–76)

These involutes or spots of time bring us to the common areas of both writers: Childhood, Time and Memory.

We normally think of the *Confessions* as being in two forms; there is the shorter, early version published as a book in 1822 one year after it had appeared in instalments in *The London Magazine*; and there is the larger, later version into which it expanded as De Quincey revised it for his collected works in 1856. But, in a way, the *Confessions* was never completed. In 1845 he began the publication in *Blackwood's* of a series of papers under the general title *Suspiria de Profundis* and the explanatory sub-title *Being a sequel to 'The Confessions of an English Opium-Eater'*. De Quincey intended to gather these new pieces into a volume without delay, for he was pleased with his work and judged it 'very greatly superior' to the original *Confessions*: 'These final *Confessions* are the *ne plus ultra* as regards the feeling and power to express it, which I can ever hope to attain.' The *Suspiria*, however, were never gathered into a volume, and in 1853, while he was extensively revising the *Confessions*, he said that 'of the *Suspiria*, not more than perhaps one third has yet been printed'. He was disappointed, too, with the enlarged *Confessions* and wondered if many readers would not prefer the book in its 'original fragmentary shape'. As a book of 'amusement' it was undoubtedly improved; 'what I doubt is, whether also as a book to *impress*'. He seems to feel that in its extended state the *Confessions* might be very much less the literature of power.

De Quincey and Wordsworth were both aware that they were attempting something new. 'It is a thing unprecedented in literary history that a man should write so much about himself', said Wordsworth of *The Prelude*; and for De Quincey the *Confessions* and *Suspiria* had 'no precedents in any literature'. The works of both writers (but especially the *Confessions*) raise the question of genre, and therefore form. Much has been written about *The Prelude* and its Epic ancestry; Wordsworth accepted and appealed to traditional literary genres, and we are rightly told that a proper understanding of his poem depends upon our understanding of *Paradise Lost* and the epic conception behind his poem.[18] If Wordsworth looked to Milton, De Quincey looked only to Wordsworth. He had no Epic ambitions and was quick to see that though Wordsworth might give the impression of writing an autobiography or memoir (the original title-page promised 'an autobiographical poem'), there were many omissions and a grand carelessness of detail which suggested that the structure of the work was not in a series of events (whether external or in the mind) chronologically related. The 'Growth of a Poet's Mind', as the sub-title described the work, was not to be a growth recorded year by year and was not to be the story of inner events subjective in manner or style. For De Quincey the shape of *The Prelude* did not lie in a narrative curve, but in the repetition of those 'spots of time' which were the structural units of the poem. These gave objectivity to subjective experience; and by cutting across time, by gathering past, present and future into one visionary object or involute, they made a structure based on the passing of calendar time unnecessary, impossible and, indeed, a lie. It is possible that De Quincey, in expanding his *Confessions* by the inclusion of more mundane passages, might have been influenced by his memory of *The Prelude*, where the 'spots of time' ('scattered everywhere' in a phrase that suggests randomness and inexplicability) retained their 'distinct pre-eminence' for the reader more strikingly when set amongst much other more low-keyed experiences. This is in part what De Quincey means by 'the principles of art which govern the movement of these *Confessions*'.

The contrast of visionary moments and everyday events

needed to be repeated in the structure of the *Confessions*. It is clear that the chronology of 'spots of time' mattered as little in the *Confessions* as in *The Prelude*; it is in Book XI (1805) that Wordsworth tells of a 'spot of time' experienced when he was only six years old; De Quincey in his later revisions and in the *Suspiria* went back to his boyhood:

> The reader who may have accompanied me in these wandering memorials of my own life and casual experiences, will be aware that in many cases the neglect of chronological order is not merely permitted, but is in fact to some degree inevitable. There are cases, for instance, which, as a whole, connect themselves with my own life at so many different eras that, upon any chronological principle of position, it would have been difficult to assign them a proper place; backwards or forwards they must have leaped, in whatever place they had been introduced; and in their entire compass, from first to last, never could have been represented as properly belonging to any one *present* time, whensoever that had been selected . . . (Masson, I, 287)

The forward and backward leap explains the position of 'spots of time' or involutes which, by dissolving the barriers of time, make of the past a perpetual present and provide both works with 'a life of logical relation'. Such moments come always 'through concrete objects' which have engaged the total attention of Wordsworth and De Quincey; and, as Wordsworth says in the powerful phrase quoted above, they have 'a vivifying virtue'. 'Vivifying' has the force of giving new life to; 'virtue' has no moral suggestion but (as defined in OED) is 'the power or operative influence in a supernatural or divine being': it is the energy of imagination. The act of attention to some object or scene, the intense act of gazing, comes from the pressure of deep feelings of fear, sorrow, joy. The 'spots of time' passage in *The Prelude* acts as an introduction to the gibbet passage, where the profound attention which creates the 'visionary dreariness' is caused by fear; the intensity of gaze is an effort to find the lost guide, but the paradox of the phrase 'visionary dreariness' suggests the transformation of the scene from fear to joy:

> In terror,
> Remembered terror, there is peace and rest.[19]

In a scene in his autobiography to which I have already
referred, De Quincey, under the contradictory emotions of
fear and pleasure, records in sharp detail the scene at the early
breakfast table before his departure without adult companion
on a long coach journey. It was not only the depth of his
feelings which gave vividness to the candles, the fire, the old
servant and the raving wind; the scene 'cleaves to my own
feelings more indelibly, from having repeatedly been concerned, either as witness or as a principal party in its little
drama'.

> Years that seem innumerable have passed since that
> December morning in my own life to which I am now recur-
> ring; and yet, even to this moment, I recollect the audible
> throbbing of heart, the leap and rushing of blood, which
> suddenly surprised me during a deep lull of the wind, when
> the aged attendant said, without hurry or agitation, but
> with something of a solemn tone, 'That is the sound of the
> wheels. I hear the chaise.' (Masson, I, 276)

When the deeply grieving young De Quincey saw his dead
sister's face, he noted unconsciously, but with visionary intensity, the bright sun, the blue sky and the sudden rising of a
warm summer wind; this combination of 'concrete objects'
that makes an involute and through which the feelings pass,
entered 'unawares' (Wordsworth's word) into his mind. In
'The Two April Mornings' it is the recurrence of the involute
of the cloud and the field of corn which gives a sudden extra
intensity to the original 'spots of time'. A year after his sister's
death De Quincey's father died; and the earlier 'spot of time'
was reinforced by a recurrence of the involute of a warm
summer's day and the apprehension of death. The episode
begins with an act of attention; the De Quincey children were
gathered on the lawn before the house for hours 'listening for
the sound of wheels'. De Quincey describes in detail the

sound of the approaching carriage 'for the sake of the undying impressions which combined themselves with the circumstances'. The 'hearse-like pace' of the carriage recalled the burial service for his sister, 'the overwhelming spectacle of that funeral which had so lately formed part in the most memorable event of my life':

> But these elements of awe . . . were for me, in my condition of morbid nervousness, raised into abiding grandeur by the antecedent experiences of that particular summer night. The listening for hours to the sounds from horses' hoofs upon distant roads, rising and falling, caught and lost . . . the peculiar solemnity of the hours succeeding to sunset – the glory of the dying day . . . the knowledge that [my father] returned only to die . . . all this chorus of restless images, or of suggestive thoughts, gave to my father's return . . . the shadowy power of an ineffaceable agency among my dreams. (Masson, I, 57–8)

In *The Prelude* 'gibbet' passage there is repetition too. Years after the first experience made vivid by fear, Wordsworth revisits the scene 'in the blessèd hours of early love'; and on the original combination of concrete objects, 'the naked pool and dreary crags', there now falls a

>   . . . radiance more divine
> From these remembrances, and from the power
> They left behind. So feeling comes in aid
> Of feeling, and diversity of strength
> Attends us, if but once we have been strong.

Repetition of an involute or spot of time brings intensification and transfiguration through memory; and in both writers memory can be described as Wordsworth describes imagination: 'the faculty which produces impressive effects out of simple elements'.

Closer still to De Quincey's experience is the episode in *The Prelude* (1805, Book XI, 345–59) when, ten days before the death of his father, Wordsworth watched for the horses that would bring him and his brothers home from school. It was a stormy day of misty rain, and the boy watched, 'straining my eyes intensely'. Round about was the involute made up of 'a naked wall', 'a single sheep', 'a whistling hawthorn' and the mist. His father's death reinforces the intensity of this spot of time. For De Quincey and Wordsworth the consequences are endless. In such moments De Quincey found 'the entire substratum' of all those dreams which later haunted him; for Wordsworth such incidents affected for ever in unknown ways 'the workings of my spirit'.

A final comparison (many others could be made) of passages from De Quincey and *The Prelude* (Book IV, 315–45) shows his indebtedness to Wordsworth in the analysis through involutes of what Wordsworth called the 'hiding places' of man's power, and also the similarities and finally the differences of that power. In the second section of 'The English Mail-Coach', 'The Vision of Sudden Death',[20] De Quincey describes a journey to Lancaster in the late night, early dawn and 'mighty calm' of a still August day. His faculties were concentrated and heightened, partly by 'the possibilities of peril' (there was always the risk of collision with other coaches) and partly by 'the peculiar solemnity and peace' of the night. In the Wordsworth passage it is the excitement of the dance and the 'slight shocks of young love-liking' that put his spirits 'on the stretch'. In both writers the separate items are observed with an attention which imposes a unity on the separate items and makes of them a spot of time.

> The sea, the atmosphere, the light, bore each an orchestral part in the universal lull. Moonlight and the first timid tremblings of the dawn were by this time blending; and the blendings were brought into a still more exquisite state of unity by a slight silvery mist, motionless and dreamy, that covered the woods and fields, but with a veil of equable transparency. (Masson, XIII, 311)

'Dreamy' is a characteristic De Quincey word; Wordsworth never uses it. But the mist, as in the Wordsworth passage, does not conceal, but *is* the unity; 'orchestral' had already suggested a whole that will be greater than the sum of the parts. Everything is distinct but nothing is separate. For

Wordsworth, as always, the spot of time will have power to erupt into the future 'with radiance more sublime'; it enshrines 'the spirit of the past for future restoration' and is supremely a source of joy:

On I walked
In blessedness, which even yet remains.

In De Quincey the vision of the dawn is followed by the superbly told moment of danger, as a collision between two fast-travelling coaches is, after moments of horror, narrowly averted. For him the spot of time did not bring joy; in this case it is followed by several 'Dream-Fugues'; recurring, dread dreams of sudden, violent death which the involute of moonlight and mist intensifies through memory.

4 Power and Knowledge

'... power, of which knowledge is the effect.'

Wordsworth

I

For De Quincey power is most richly revealed in language which incarnates thought. Knowledge is dressed in language; power is incarnate in words and speaks through them. Between power and knowledge, between the literature of power and the literature of knowledge, there is a great gulf fixed, an 'indispensable schism'. De Quincey owed this famous distinction to Wordsworth, as, indeed, he claimed (incorrectly) that he owed all his critical notions to Wordsworth: 'For which distinction, as for most sound criticism on poetry, or any subject connected with it that I have ever met with, I must acknowledge my obligations to many years' conversation with Mr. Wordsworth.'[1] We may assume that Wordsworth had more to say about this distinction in some of his talk with De Quincey, for the written evidence is slight. It comes in the *Essay, Supplementary to the Preface* of 1815. Wordsworth there insists that the loftiest aim of literature, 'that dominion over the spirits of readers by which they are to be humbled and humanised, in order that they may be purified and exalted', will never be attained by 'the mere communication of *Knowledge*'. But the word 'taste', as a critical term, continually implies the opposite: 'It is a metaphor, taken from a *passive* sense of the human body, and transferred to things which are in their essence *not* passive.' When the word is used in criticism of literature or painting it produces an inversion in the order of things 'whereby a passive faculty is made paramount among the faculties conversant with the fine arts'. The faculty

76

of taste may be trusted in comment on such formal matters as 'proportion or congruity':

> But the profound and the exquisite in feeling, the lofty and universal in thought and imagination; or, in ordinary language, the pathetic and the sublime; – are neither of them, accurately speaking, objects of a faculty which could ever without a sinking in the spirit of Nations have been designated by the metaphor – *Taste*. And why? Because without the exertion of a co-operating *power* in the mind of the Reader, there can be no adequate sympathy with either of these emotions: without this auxiliary impulse, elevated or profound passion cannot exist.[2]

In spite of the italicised *power* the point is not yet quite clear, for the power he speaks of must already be in the reader before the power of the pathetic or sublime can move him. Power will call forth power; deep will speak only to deep; only by a co-operative grace can the voice of art be heard. But a little later, while still implying that in a vital sense the good writer makes the good reader, that the power of the word can be ignited only by contact with the reader, Wordsworth gives more clearly to the word 'power' the meaning which De Quincey adopted and elaborated. 'And this brings us to the point':

> If every great poet with whose writings men are familiar, in the highest exercise of his genius, before he can be thoroughly enjoyed, has to call forth and to communicate *power*, this service, in a still greater degree, falls upon an original writer, at his first appearance in the world . . . Of genius, in the fine arts, the only infallible sign is the widening of the sphere of human sensibility . . . Genius is the application of powers to objects on which they had not before been exercised, or the employment of them in such a manner as to produce effects hitherto unknown.

The reader cannot passively acquire new insights and experiences as he can passively acquire mere knowledge; 'to create taste is to call forth and bestow power, of which knowledge is the effect'.[3]

De Quincey was more interested in the power bestowed than in the power called forth; but from these few hints (and no doubt also from things said in the 'many years' conversation with Mr. Wordsworth') he built a substantial theory of criticism. It was a structure which was never much attended to and which continues to be ignored. Helen Darbishire said long ago that the current neglect of the theory proved its success. 'We do not need to be told,' she said, 'that books are of two kinds, those that communicate knowledge and those that communicate power.' We do not need to be told this, it seems, because De Quincey's insight is now a commonplace and no one cares about its origin:

> Yet in De Quincey's day these ideas were by no means commonly understood or accepted, and it is his distinction to have set forth with clearness and force a theory which Coleridge only vaguely implied, and Wordworth never elaborated in his writing.[4]

But the truth probably is that the word 'imagination' as Wordsworth and Coleridge used it is very similar to De Quincey's power, and that the authority of the two poets gave to their term a currency which De Quincey's could not manage. Imagination had also the advantage of being a familiar word; Coleridge might confuse the issue for many readers, but at least they began with familiar ground under their feet. De Quincey very seldom uses the word 'imagination', and never in any attempt to establish a critical theory or make any critical distinction. He says nothing about Coleridge's discussion of imagination, although Coleridge's definitions (or some of them) and his distinction between imagination and fancy were close to De Quincey's own definition of power and the distinction between the literature of power and the literature of knowledge. For Coleridge, imagination 'dissolves, diffuses, dissipates, in order to recreate . . . It is essentially *vital*, even as all objects (*as* objects) are essentially fixed and dead. FANCY, on the contrary, has no other counters to play with, but fixities and definities'.[5] Fancy, like Wordsworth's taste, is a passive faculty. In the 1815 'Preface' and the *Essay, Supplementary* Wordsworth's comments on imagination stress its activity, its creative power; and he frequently insists, as De Quincey does, that the imagination works most effectively through imagery. 'In an image,' says Wordsworth, the 'processes of imagination' give to an object 'a new existence'; it 'shapes and *creates*'. For De Quincey, poetic metaphor brings together his views on power and incarnation, and like Wordsworth, he italicises its creativity:

> Imagery is sometimes not the mere apparelling of a thought, and of a nature to be detached from the thought, but is the coefficient that, being superadded to something else, absolutely *makes* the thought as a *third* and separate existence. (Masson, X, 262)

As Wordsworth said, imagination 'bestows power of which knowledge is the effect'. De Quincey will distinguish between the felt knowledge which is born from the workings of imagination, and the ordinary passive knowledge which deals in separates and is merely a mode of memory. Even when imagination and power are not mentioned, the indebtedness of De Quincey to Wordsworth is striking. When Wordsworth says that through poetry, truth is 'carried alive into the heart by passion', he defines the operation of both faculties.

Why should De Quincey have picked up and extended Wordsworth's brief use of power and (with all his reverence for the poet) have glaringly avoided all discussion of imagination? The answer may be that Wordsworth's brief flirtation with the critical term power in the *Essay, Supplementary* stemmed from his own temporary dissatisfaction with the word imagination which seemed at the moment too vague and too old a term to have either precision or impact. Like taste (he reminds his readers), 'IMAGINATION is a word which has been forced to extend its services far beyond the point to which philosophy would have confined them'; it has been 'overstrained'. Indeed, 'poverty of language is the primary cause of the use which we make of the word, Imagination'. The master had dropped an alternative term, power, and the disciple, because of his reverence, picked it up.

II

De Quincey's first explanation of the terms power and knowledge appeared eight years after Wordsworth's 1815 'Preface'
and *Essay* in the third of five 'Letters to a Young Man whose
Education has been Neglected' published in the *London
Magazine* in 1823. He was later to restate and amplify the
theory, but this early definition is shorter and simpler. 'The
word *literature* is a perpetual source of confusion because it is
used in two senses' which are commonly confused. Properly
speaking, 'Literature is the direct and adequate antithesis of
Books of Knowledge'; but in common parlance, dictionaries,
grammars, almanacs, Parliamentary reports and treatises on
billiards are also called literature. This says De Quincey is, of
course, ludicrous, but even books with higher pretensions
must be denied the title of literature; 'as, for instance, books of
voyages and travels, and generally all books in which the
matter to be communicated is paramount to the manner or
form of its communication'. It will be difficult to construct the
idea of literature with accuracy, or always to know what to
include or exclude; for literature is 'the supreme fine art, and
liable to the difficulties which attend such a subtle notion'.
Most readers assume that the opposite of books of knowledge
is books which give pleasure; that books either instruct or
amuse. They are wrong:

> The true antithesis to knowledge, in this case, is not *pleasure*,
> but *power*. All that is literature seeks to communicate power;
> all that is not literature, to communicate knowledge. Now,
> if it be asked what is meant by communicating power, I, in
> my turn, would ask by what name a man would designate
> the case in which I should be made to feel vividly, and with
> a vital consciousness, emotions which ordinary life rarely or
> never supplies occasions for exciting, and which had pre-
> viously lain unwakened, and hardly within the dawn of
> consciousness – as myriads of modes of feeling are at this
> moment in every human mind for want of a poet to organize
> them? I say, when these inert and sleeping forms *are* organ-
> ized, when these possibilities *are* actualized, is the conscious

and living possession of mine *power*, or what is it? (Masson, X, 48)

(Wordsworth's insistence on 'the co-operating *power* in the mind of the Reader' has shrunk a little to the capacity for anamnesis, to the ability to awaken 'inert and sleeping forms' in our consciousness.) When, in *King Lear*, the height and depth of human passion are revealed to us, and we are 'suddenly startled into a feeling of the infinity of the world' within us, this is power, 'or what may I call it?' Wordsworth would have answered, imagination: that which gives to human passion 'a pathos and a spirit which shall re-admit them like revelations of the moment'. *Paradise Lost*, for example, communicates power; 'a pretension far above all communication of knowledge':

Henceforth, therefore, I shall use the antithesis power and knowledge as the most philosophical expression for literature (that is, Literae Humaniores) and anti-literature (that is, Literae didacticae). (Masson, X, 49)

De Quincey at once tries to clarify his meaning by suggesting that the literature of power (De Quincey is thinking of poetry, and, as always, includes in the term any example of impassioned prose) is untranslateable. Coleridge had already talked of poetry's *untranslateablenesss* in words of the same language without injury to the meaning'. De Quincey agrees; but 'all knowledge is translateable, and translateable without one atom of loss'.

In these 1823 *Letters to a Young Man* the description of power is still sketchy, and its difference from knowledge is nowhere linked to the view of language as incarnation. But the antithetic terms power and knowledge were now part of De Quincey's inevitable vocabulary; he pondered them, and over the next quarter of a century repeatedly used them (without much attempt at explanation) as useful shorthand terms for the discussion not only of literature but of many other topics as well. In 1830, in an essay on Kant, he states in parenthesis that literature in its 'finer departments' offers 'power and not knowledge'. In 1838 he finds the principal fault of Charles Lamb's drama *John Woodvil* to be 'defect of power', and suggests that power is close to 'creative energy'. In 1840, in a series of papers called 'The Essences', he says that

> The Christian Religion offers two things: a body of truth of things to be believed, in the first place; in the second place, a spiritual agency . . . for carrying these truths into operative life. Otherwise expressed, the Christian Religion offers – 1st, a knowledge, 2nd, a power: that is, 1st, a rudder to guide, 2nd, sails to propel. (Masson, VII, 167).

De Quincey continued to use these terms for the rest of his life. In a very late autobiographical essay (1853) they appear in a way which assumes the reader's understanding of their total meanings, and he warns that 'the limiting idea of knowledge' must not be 'confounded with the infinite idea of power'.

In 1848 De Quincey restated and amplified his theory of power and knowledge in two essays, 'Oliver Goldsmith' and 'The Poetry of Pope'.[6] In the Goldsmith essay he wants the word literature to be used in one sense only; not for 'the mere literature of knowledge', but for the literature of power. (In 1823 he had avoided the ambiguity or confusion of the word literature by referring to 'Books of knowledge' as the proper antithesis to literature.) The word power must be used for literature that 'speaks to what is genial in man, viz. to the human *spirit*, and *not* for literature (falsely so called) as it speaks to the meagre understanding'. He finds that a change has taken place in the previous generation; literature (and, indeed, all the arts) 'have now come to be regarded rather as powers that are to mould than as luxuries that are to embellish'.[7]

A few months later, in the essay on Pope, he had much more to say. Pope raised the problem sharply because he was, in the ordinary phrase, a didactic poet; and didacticism suggests a book of knowledge that speaks to the meagre or insulated understanding. The essay is a defence of Pope, though a defence of an embarrassed kind. For most contemporary readers in 1848 Pope was that dreadful thing, a satiric poet. Yes, he was, agrees De Quincey, but he was much more. Had he been 'merely a satiric poet' (the 'merely' suggests difficulty ahead) he would have sacrificed 'much of the splendour' which, for De Quincey, still 'surrounds him in our traditional estimate of his merit'. (The pronoun 'our' is simply De Quincey's way of referring to himself in magazine articles and does not imply a common or generally held opinion of Pope.) The defence of Pope needs a return to a basic question: 'what is it that we mean by *literature*?' The best way to answer is not by attempting to define literature, but by reaching 'a sharper distinction of the two functions which it fulfils'. The distinction now is not absolute as it was in 1823; 'the two separate offices' of literature 'may blend and often *do* do', but they can also be totally separate from each other and, indeed, are 'naturally fitted for reciprocal repulsion'. The function of the literature of knowledge (De Quincey does not return to the earlier phrase, books of knowledge) is 'to teach': the function of the literature of power is, 'to move: the first is a rudder; the second, an oar or a sail'. The literature of knowledge 'speaks to the *mere* discursive understanding'; the literature of power speaks ultimately to 'the higher understanding or reason, but always through affections of pleasure and sympathy'; it must occupy itself with 'human passions, desires, and genial emotions'. Both kinds of literature are concerned with truth; but 'there is a rarer thing than truth, – namely, *power*, or deep sympathy with truth'.

What do you learn from 'Paradise Lost'? Nothing at all. What do you learn from a cookery-book? Something new, something that you did not know before, in every paragraph. But would you therefore put the wretched cookery-book on a higher level of estimation than the divine poem? What you owe to Milton is not any knowledge, of which a million separate items are still but a million of advancing steps on the same early level; what you owe is *power*, – that is, exercise and expansion to your own latent capacity of sympathy with the infinite . . . *All* the steps of knowledge, from first to last, carry you further on the same plane, but could never raise you one foot above your ancient level of earth: whereas the very *first* step in power is a flight – is an ascending movement into another element where earth is forgotten. (Masson, XI, 55–6)

De Quincey neatly escapes from the dilemma that has already dogged him of having books of knowledge and literature of knowledge. A cookery-book, a book of knowledge, can be destroyed or lost. Newton's *Principia*, a mighty instance of the literature of knowledge, may be superseded, but not destroyed. When another scientist 'builds higher upon the foundations laid by this book, he throws it . . . into decay and darkness'. He 'superannuates' Newton's book, but 'by weapons won from this book'; so that Newton's work 'has transmigrated into other forms'. It is the ideas of Newton that have allowed him even this shadowy continued existence; it is the translateability of his words which, in whatever language they appear, can appeal only to the intellectual faculty, that has denied them any further force. A cookery-book, a grammar or a treatise on billiards cannot have even this immortality by proxy; they are merely 'provisional' books upon trial and sufferance, and, 'like the fashions of this world', pass away.

Now, on the contrary, the Iliad, the Prometheus of Aeschylus, the Othello or King Lear, the Hamlet or Macbeth, and the Paradise Lost, are . . . triumphant for ever as long as the languages exist in which they speak or can be taught to speak. They never *can* transmigrate into new incarnations. (Masson, XI, 57)

Their power is incarnate in their language. De Quincey, in fact, allows one form of transmigration for the literature of power, one way in which it may continue with, perhaps, undiminished force to move us. This is when great poetry is translated into great poetry. Chaucer's *Tales*, 'never equalled on this earth for their tenderness' have power in 'the language of their natal day' and also 'in the modernisations of Dryden, of Pope, and Wordsworth'; but with what diminution of power De Quincey does not say.

In 1823 De Quincey (as we have seen) rejected the notion of

a *literature* of knowledge, and called such writings 'anti-literature (that is, Literae didacticae)'. His first essay on Pope, published in 1838 in the seventh edition of *Encyclopaedia Britannica*, scarcely raised the question of didactic poetry. In it Pope is intelligently and selectively praised: *The Rape of the Lock* is 'the most exquisite monument of playful fancy that universal literature offers'; the 'immortal *Dunciad*' (no trans-migration needed) is 'profoundly poetic', and 'the very great-est of Pope's works, – a monument of satirical power the greatest which man has produced'. He thinks less highly of Pope's overtly didactic works: the *Essay on Man* is much inferior to *The Dunciad*, and the *Essay on Criticism* ('very unreasonably' considered his best performance) is nothing better than 'a collection of independent maxims . . . having no natural order or logical dependency'. (He does not yet see them as 'anti-literature'.) The *Moral Epistles* and *Imitations of Horace*, which might seem a more difficult challenge to De Quincey's views on knowledge and power, are not discussed. Pope, however, is 'a great poet', and 'for qualities the very same as belong to his most distinguished brethren . . . for impassioned thinking, powerful description, pathetic reflec-tion, brilliant narration'. The several phrases, as De Quincey implies, could with equal truth be used of Wordsworth. Pope differs from his peers only because 'he carried these powers into a different field, and moved chiefly amongst the social paths of men'.

In the 1848 essay on Pope, the still later essay, 'Lord Car-lisle on Pope', 1851, and a postscript added in 1858 (a year before his death), De Quincey returns to the problem of Pope. Pope is still a great poet. *The Dunciad* is profoundly prophetic and is still his greatest poem; but the *Essay on Man* is now Pope's worst work: it has 'no central principle' and therefore no 'coherency among the separate thoughts'. The *Moral Epis-tles* are bad because they aren't satire at all, but 'arose in a sense of talent for caustic effects, unsupported by any satiric heart'. Because Pope (and Dryden) deal with 'the contempla-tion of society and manners' (those 'social paths of men' which in 1823 made no difference) their work is now 'a minor key of literature'. Pope's passion is not 'the creating passion' of Shakespeare, but a mere 'reflecting and recombining passion', the product of 'fancy, and the habit of minute distinction'. *The Dunciad* is a great poem, is literature of power. But *The Dunciad* is a satiric poem; satire is didactic, therefore 'anti-literature' and cannot be literature of power. De Quincey, faced with this contradiction, is forced to consider the whole question of didactic literature.

He begins dogmatically. 'What is didactic poetry? . . . The predicate destroys the subject.' Didactic poetry as ordinarily understood is a contradiction in terms; but why should we ordinarily understand it so? Wordsworth had suggested a richer meaning in 1800. He says of his poems in *Lyrical Ballads* that

> each of them has a worthy *purpose*. Not that I mean to say that I always began to write with a distinct purpose formally conceived; but I believe that my habits of meditation have so formed my feelings, as that my descriptions of such objects as strongly excite those feelings will be found to carry along with them a *purpose*.

Poems by indirection will find direction out; the truly didactic is inseparable from the feelings in a state of excitement, and the purpose has to be borne along by the feelings. The real purposes of poems, De Quincey agrees, must be 'immanent'; they must be 'hidden in their poems': hidden and yet discoverable; discoverable through indirection:

> Poetry, or any one of the fine arts (all of which alike speak through the genial nature of man and his excited sensibilities), can teach only as nature teaches, – viz. by deep impulse, by hieroglyphic suggestion. Their teaching is not direct or explicit, but lurking, implicit, masked in deep incarnations. To teach formally and professedly is to abandon the very differential character and principle of poetry. If poetry could condescend to teach anything, it would be truths moral or religious. But even these it can utter only through symbols and actions. The great moral, for instance, the last result, of the Paradise Lost is once formally announced, viz. *to justify the ways of God to man*; but it teaches itself only by diffusing its lesson through the entire poem in

the total succession of events and purposes; and even this succession teaches it only when the whole is gathered into unity by a reflex act of meditation . . . (Masson, XI, 88–9)

Didactic poetry can be successful, is able to *be* poetry, only when what it teaches is revealed in the incarnations of language, symbol and total shape or structure. The unity is greater than the sum of the parts and dictates their final meaning; the whole work is the final incarnation which dissolves the contradictions that had seemed to lie in the very term, didactic poetry. The total work is the literature of power, 'of which knowledge is the effect'. Didactic poetry, like other poetry, speaks to 'the understanding heart'.

This 'properly didactic function' is something quite different from instruction; 'what we are denying is that the element of instruction enters *at all* into didactic poetry'. A poet, indeed, may intend to instruct and may think that he is instructing, but he is either misleading or misled. First of all, to instruct is 'to address the *insulated* understanding', and that is 'to lay aside the Prospero's robe of poetry'. But there is a second and more practical objection to any suggestion that poetry should instruct, and that is the sheer needless difficulty and clumsiness of poetry for the purpose. If a man's real reason in writing a poem were to instruct, 'by what suggestion of idiocy should he choose to begin by putting on fetters . . . of metre, and perhaps of rhyme'. A poem, by its very shortness (and even if it is a long poem), must be eclectic; it cannot give all the details needed for adequate instruction; and even if it could, the poet would find many of them irresistibly unpoetic. 'The subject of the Georgics, for instance, is Rural Economy as practised by Italian farmers; but Virgil not only *omits* altogether innumerable points of instruction', but does not trouble to make intelligible any which he happens to mention. 'He pretends to give you a lecture on farming, in order to have an excuse for carrying you all round the beautiful farm.' The poet always has to select; 'so far from *teaching*, he presupposes the reader already *taught*, in order that he may go along with the movement of the descriptions'.[8] So do not believe a poet when he tells you that he wishes to instruct. Never trust the artist; trust the tale. Pope in the *Essay on Criticism* and Horace in the *Epistola ad Pisones* may have believed themselves to be 'the professional expounders . . . of the grounds and theory of critical rules applied to poetic composition'. But Lawrence's dictum takes an early form in De Quincey: 'No matter if they did. Nobody was less likely to understand their own purposes than themselves.' Their real purposes must be sought in the poems and not from the poets:

> We cannot possibly allow a man to argue upon the meaning or tendency of his own book, as against the evidence of the book itself. The book is unexceptionable authority; and, as against *that* the author has no *locus standi*.[9]

Literature thus has power to teach through man's 'sensibilities'. Its teaching is not direct but 'implicit, masked in deep incarnations'. It speaks through 'symbols' and 'the total succession of events'; but it can still teach only when these many things become one in the unity of the completed work. De Quincey seems to say that literature can teach only through style, but only when he gives to style 'the largest meaning of that word':

> that is, for the mode of presenting a subject, of effecting the transitions and connexions . . . for the arts of preparation, of recapitulation, of peroration, together with the whole world of refinements which belong to a beautiful and impressive diction. (Masson, VIII, 91)

But already in this very early (1830) definition of style, the word seems to be taking on a possible other meaning. Phrases like 'mode of presenting' and 'refinements' hint at a more external or mechanical view of style than De Quincey offers. And this is the difficulty: De Quincey uses the term in two different ways, and even in one paragraph he can move from one meaning to the other. At one moment style is very close to the total incarnation of the author's meaning; at another, style is close to De Quincey's definition of rhetoric and can 'yield a separate intellectual pleasure quite apart from the interest of the subject treated'. The two meanings exist today as they existed in 1830; De Quincey knew of the two separate meanings and in his article on 'Style' (1840–41) he described them:[10]

> The word *style* has with us a twofold meaning: one, the narrow meaning, expressing the mere *synthesis onomaton*, the syntaxis or combination of words into sentences; the other of far wider extent, and expressing all possible relations that can arise between thoughts and words – the total effect of a writer as derived from manner. Style may be viewed as an *organic* thing and as a *mechanic* thing. (Masson, X, 163)

Organic style belongs to the literature of power; 'it propagates the communicated power without loss'. A mechanic style is not 'an organ of thought' but considers merely the way in which 'words act upon words, and through a particular grammar'. De Quincey says that 'style is the subtlest of subjects' and that it is therefore important not to confound the two functions. But what he says here and elsewhere on style is confusing because he conducts a defence of both meanings simultaneously, and because his twofold meaning becomes threefold as style veers towards his descriptions of rhetoric.

More usually, however, when De Quincey talks of style he means organic style, the total effect of a writer, the communication of power which comes from the ability of 'the thinking faculty to connect itself with the feeling, and with the creative faculty of the imagination'. It follows that in such communication content and style cannot be considered apart; the matter of a book is not distinct from the manner or capable of a 'separate insulation', for the one is 'embedded, entangled and interfused through the other' and bids defiance to 'gross mechanical separations'. The tendency to view the two as separate is still very common and, indeed, not entirely mistaken, since there are many subjects for which the question of style (in the organic sense) will be inappropriate and even unnecessary: 'Physics, for example, in some of its numerous branches; mathematics; or some great standing problem of metaphysics.' In these cases 'one rule of good taste' will be 'to reject all ornaments of style whatever – in fact all style'. (The sudden shift from 'ornaments of style' to 'all style' shows how easily De Quincey moves from discussion of style as organic to style as a form of rhetoric.) However, he recovers himself and makes his position clear: 'unless on a question which admits some action of the feelings, in a business of pure understanding, style, properly defined, is impossible'.[11]

The passing of time makes little change to De Quincey's opinion. Nine years later, in 1840, the same point is amplified. 'A man who has absolute facts to communicate from some branch of study external to himself . . . is independent of style . . . the matter transcends and oppresses the manner.'

> But he who has to treat a vague question . . . where everything is to be finished out of his own peculiar feelings, or his own way of viewing things . . . soon finds that the manner of treating it not only transcends the matter, but very often, and in a very great proportion, *is* the matter.

This will be particularly true of 'subjective exercises of the mind'. In meditative poetry, for example,

> the problem before the writer is to project his own inner mind; to bring out consciously what yet lurks by involution in many unanalysed feelings . . . to pass through a prism and radiate into distinct elements . . . Now, in such cases, the skill with which detention or conscious arrest is given to the evanescent, external projection to what is internal, outline to what is fluxionary, and body to what is vague, – all this depends entirely on the command over language as the one sole means of embodying ideas; and in such cases the style, or, in the largest sense, *manner*, is confluent with the matter. (Masson, X, 226–7)

There is here, as in other places, the same ambiguity in the word 'language'. Is it vocabulary, or is it the whole 'manner of treating' a subject? The ambiguity is not resolved a few lines later when De Quincey endorses Wordsworth's remark on language as 'the incarnation of thoughts' and not 'the dress of thoughts', by calling it 'by far the weightiest thing we ever heard on the subject of style'; for 'style' in the same sentence shifts to 'language or diction' where the 'or' is probably conjunctive.

But, generally speaking, you can no more deal thus with poetic thoughts than you can with soul and body. The union is too subtle, the intertexture too ineffable, – each co-existing not merely *with* the other, but *in* and through the other. (Masson, X, 230)

Later in the same essay one of the functions of style is 'to regenerate the normal *power* and impressiveness of a subject which has become dormant to the sensibilities'. Wordsworth through imagination was 'to give the power of novelty to things of everyday'; for De Quincey, through style 'decaying lineaments are to be retraced and faded colouring to be refreshed'. Among 'the possible gifts of style' are 'light to *see* the road, power to *advance along* it'.

Style as 'a mechanic thing' can sometimes sound very mechanic indeed. At one time it can mean simply 'the construction of sentences' and 'the logic' that connects one sentence to another; De Quincey refers to 'the science of style considered as a machine' and says that it can 'brighten the *intelligibility* of a subject which is obscure to the understanding'. At another time style is something closer to sleight-of-hand; its aim is to contrive

the best forms for appearing to say something new when in reality you are but echoing yourself; to break up massy chords into running variations; and to mask, by slight differences in the manner, a virtual identity in the substance. (Masson, X, 140)

Style is here 'the proper technical discipline' for familiarising the mind with 'a startling or a complex novelty'. Finally the mechanic style can sometimes be very unmechanic; it can be something close to De Quincey's description of rhetoric, something which can, after all, be considered by itself, a manner and 'magic of language' independent (almost) of matter, and a separate and 'exquisite art'.

It is certain that style, or (to speak by the most general expression) the management of language, ranks amongst the fine arts, and is able therefore to yield a separate intellectual pleasure quite apart from the interest of the subject treated. So far it is already one error to rate the value of style as if it were necessarily a secondary or subordinate thing. On the contrary, style has an *absolute* value, like the product of any other exquisite art, quite distinct from the value of the subject about which it is employed, and irrelatively to the subject; precisely as the fine workmanship of Scopas the Greek, or of Cellini the Florentine, is equally valued by the connoisseur, whether embodied in bronze or marble, in an ivory or a golden vase. (Masson, X, 260)

Style has shrunk from power to taste; it is not simply a 'separate intellectual pleasure' that style now offers, but a separate aesthetic pleasure; a passive pleasure that does not engage with the feelings or with what De Quincey elsewhere calls 'the creative faculty of imagination'. De Quincey wants to sustain two opposite meanings of style at the same time. In England, he complains, we make a double mistake; we believe that matter and manner are separate things, and then we despise the manner. This 'fine art' of style with its 'absolute value' is of small account with us. Our tendency is to 'degrade the value of the ornamental' in favour of 'the substantial or grossly useful'; yet this 'rarest and most intellectual art' is finest when disinterested, when 'most conspicuously detached from gross palpable uses'. But, says De Quincey, style often 'really *has* the obvious uses of that gross palpable order' when it circulates 'the life-blood of sensibility' into 'an old set of truths'. The word style threatens to collapse (its usefulness is certainly obscured) under the weight of opposing meanings which De Quincey heaps on it. He was wise to take up and renovate the word rhetoric.

III

He develops the term as a protest against the prevailing English distrust, neglect and undervaluing of style; his quarrel, he says, is 'co-extensive with that general principle in England which tends in all things to set the matter above the manner, the substance above the external show'.

In no country upon earth, were it possible to carry such a maxim into practical effect, is it a more determinate tendency of the national mind to value the *matter* of a book not only as paramount to the *manner*, but even as distinct from it, and as capable of a separate insulation. (Masson, X, 137)

Nearly twenty years before Matthew Arnold employed the terms Hebraism and Hellenism De Quincey used the more simple words Greek and Hebrew to explain and attack the English failure to appreciate style as a fine art. Arnold is the more impressive; his greater sympathy with Greek thought allowed him to define Hellenism as 'an unclouded clearness of mind, an unimpeded play of thought'. Hebraism is a practical moral energy, and Arnold calls his distinction 'only another version of the old story that energy is our strong point and favourable characteristic rather than intelligence'. The human spirit must proceed 'by the idea of a comprehensive adjustment of the claims of both the sides in man, the moral as well as the intellectual, of a full estimate of both, and of a reconciliation of both'. De Quincey's profound admiration for Greek Drama did not always extend to Greek philosophy, and his animus against Plato is notorious and absurd. His tone, it is true, can sometimes sound like Arnold's:

In Athens, the question before the public assembly was, peace or war – before our House of Commons, perhaps the Exchequer Bills Bill; at Athens, a league or no league – in England, the Tithe of Agistment Commutation-Bills Renewal Bill; in Athens – shall we forgive a ruined enemy? in England – shall we cancel the tax on farthing rushlights? (Masson, X, 340)

But, in fact, De Quincey's mockery is used in a less serious cause; what he appeals for is something smaller than Hellenism, for an aesthetic appreciation of style as a fine art. The insistence of the English on matter as separate from manner and superior to it, though it may make it hard for them to understand how the language of literature works, is 'a principle noble in itself'. Greece was, says De Quincey, 'too ebullient with intellectual activity';

> so that the opposite pole of the mind, which points to the
> mysterious and the spiritual, was, in the agile Greek, too
> intensely a child of the earth, starved and palsied; whilst in
> the Hebrew, dull and inert intellectually, but in his spiritual
> organs awake and sublime, the case was precisely reversed.
> Yet, after all, the result was immeasurably in favour of the
> Hebrew. (Masson, X, 250)

De Quincey's early essay on 'Rhetoric' (1828), which was
intended to correct the English bias against the manner or
style of a book as one of the fine arts, in fact merely helped to
confirm it. Donald Davie[12] has recently reminded us that the
words 'decoration' and 'decorative' are still pejorative:

> It was Wordsworth and Coleridge 180 years ago who tried
> to separate poetry from rhetoric; and their endeavour
> throws a long shadow over the Romantic and post-
> Romantic generations of the present day.

Yes; and De Quincey helped them. He considers and rejects
the two popular views of rhetoric. The first is that rhetoric is
the treatment of a subject 'with more than usual gaiety of
conscious ornament'; as such its aim is not to win assent but
'to stimulate the attention and captivate the taste'. The second is that it has to do with argument; its aim is to persuade or
convince, and 'it applies itself more specifically to a definite
purpose of utility, viz. fraud'. De Quincey proposes a third
definition which excludes the other two. 'Where conviction
begins the field of Rhetoric ends . . . and as to the passions, we
contend that they are not within the province of Rhetoric, but
of Eloquence.' This is brisk but not clear. Slowly the exclusion
of the two traditional definitions becomes less firm; and
eloquence, which is here thrown out of the window, tends
from time to time to come back in at the door.

At first De Quincey shows the difference between eloquence
and rhetoric to be clear and absolute:

> By Eloquence we understand the overflow of powerful feel-
> ings upon occasions fitted to excite them. But Rhetoric is

the art of aggrandizing and bringing out into strong relief, by means of various and striking thoughts, some aspect of truth which of itself is supported by no spontaneous feelings, and therefore rests upon artificial aids. (Masson, X, 92)

The phrase from Wordsworth's 'Preface' makes eloquence indistinguishable from De Quincey's idea of poetry, and it invokes confusingly the notions of spontaneity and (in contrast with rhetoric) of sincerity. Rhetoric, on the other hand, is art, though of an inferior kind; it is the art, as David Masson calls it, 'of a conscious playing with a subject intellectually and inventively'. Rhetoric rests on 'artificial aids'; it is exaggeration, a game in which the feelings have no part. Eloquence may be something separate, but even as he makes his distinction it remains for De Quincey the greater quality. Scarcely an example of Shakespeare's rhetoric is to be found 'which does not pass by fits into a higher element of eloquence or poetry'. Eloquence emerges as another word for power (a De Quincey distinction without difference). It seems now as if the highest rhetoric tends towards eloquence; yet in the work of Jeremy Taylor there is an 'everlasting strife and fluctuation between his rhetoric and eloquence', and this strife is (confusingly) what makes Taylor (with Sir Thomas Browne) 'the richest, the most dazzling . . . of all rhetoricians'. Truth-telling is not the prime aim of rhetoric, but only 'some aspect of truth'; 'the province of rhetoric . . . lies amongst that vast field of cases where there is a *pro* and a *con*, with the chance of right and wrong, true and false, distributed in varying proportions between them'. Rhetoric gives us a splinter of truth. The rhetorician exhibits his arts and puts us in possession of a 'one-sided estimate by giving an impulse to one side and by withdrawing the mind from all thoughts or images which support the other'.[13] Yet 'the artifice and machinery of rhetoric furnishes in its degree as legitimate a basis for intellectual pleasure as any other'. Lord Bacon, for example, had 'great advantages for rhetoric' but is not a rhetorician:

The reason is that, being always in quest of absolute truth, he contemplates all subjects, not through the rhetorical

fancy, which is most excited by mere seeming resemblances
. . . but through the philosophic fancy, or that which rests
upon real analogies. (Masson, X, 109)

The word 'fancy' in this sentence has two nearly opposite
meanings (this time perhaps De Quincey offers difference
without distinction). But the difference is very close to
Wordsworth's. Bacon cannot be a rhetorician because he contemplates all subjects through real analogies, that is, imagination; his search for truth has nothing to do with the 'mere
seeming resemblances' of fancy. A 'pure rhetorician' sees
fancy as self-sustained from its own activities and as the 'conscious and profuse lavishing of ornaments' for mere purposes
of effect.

De Quincey's views on rhetoric are a far cry from Wordsworth's endeavour 'to look steadily at my subject'; yet it is
perhaps the influence of Wordsworth which inhibits the more
single-minded development of a theory or rhetoric. It is the
pressure of Wordsworth's example which leads De Quincey to
hive off rhetoric from eloquence and to attempt the paradoxical aims of trying to bring about a restoration and revaluation
of rhetoric as a fine art, while conceding all the time its
inferiority to eloquence, to power, to the Wordsworthian
example. De Quincey's aim was to check the split between
rhetoric and poetry: his attempt confirmed it.

De Quincey begins his essay by rejecting the notion of
rhetoric as the treatment of a subject with 'more than usual
gaiety of conscious ornament' which captivates the taste; but
in fact, he often confounds it with his alternative description of
rhetoric as tending nowhere, with no function, a self-conscious
display, a splendid end in itself. Rhetoric is like *'bravura*, as
being intentionally a passage of display and elaborate execution'. It is 'playing gracefully' with those arguments only
which could promise 'a brilliant effect'. It is like

a histrionic fencing match, where the object of the actor is
not in good earnest to put his antagonist to the sword, but
to exhibit a few elegant passes in *carte* and *tierce*, not forget-
ting the secondary object of displaying to advantage any
diamonds and rubies that may chance to scintillate upon
his sword-hand.[14]

Rhetoric is like a fireworks display and affords ingenuity, skill and delight for the eye. 'All rhetoric is a mode of pyrotechny, and all pyrotechnics are by necessity fugitive, yet even in these frail pomps there are many degrees of frailty.' But all rhetoric, 'like all flesh, is partly unreal, and the glory of both is fleeting'. Rhetoric is 'an art rejoicing in its own energies'. Energies, De Quincey feels, as a more neutral word than power, better describes and circumscribes rhetoric which can effervesce or glitter or change colour, but cannot move beyond itself. The rhetorician hangs upon his own thoughts 'as an object of conscious interest, to play with them, to watch and pursue them through a maze of inversions, evolutions, and harlequin changes'. There are times, even, when rhetoric, for decorum's sake, ought to be nothing other than aesthetic display. De Quincey rebuked a friend who admired a gold sovereign for being 'elegantly simple':

> 'And *that*, weak-minded friend, is exactly the thing which a coin ought not to be: the duty of a golden coin is to be as florid as it can, rich with Corinthian ornaments, and as gorgeous as a peacock's tail.' So of rhetoric. (Masson, X, 130)

Yet not always so of rhetoric; his sprightly comments are shadowed by, nudged by qualification. The object of rhetoric is not always to be as gorgeous as a peacock's tail; and even the fireworks of rhetoric can stand in '*some* degree of relation to the permanencies of truth'. Not all the 'glitterings of rhetoric' are 'washed on from the outside', but can sometimes be 'worked into the texture'. Rhetoric is, indeed, 'ornaments of style', but it is primarily 'the management of the thoughts'. The qualifications and change of emphasis are forced on De Quincey by his vast admiration for Burke and for such seventeenth-century prose-writers as Sir Thomas Browne, Jeremy Taylor and John Donne. The imagery in French rhetoric may be merely ornamental; 'as if formed from fulminating powder it expires in the very act of birth'. The imagery of the great English rhetoricians extends, amplifies and fortifies the thought 'by some indirect argument of its truth'.

Every species of composition, says De Quincey, is to be judged by its own laws. The 'artifice and machinery of rhetoric' provide as legitimate an intellecual pleasure as any other; of 'an inferior' order, it is true, but 'it cannot impeach the excellence of an epigram that it is not a tragedy'. It is De Quincey's search for the profounder truth of tragedy (or the 'absolute truth' which Bacon sought) and not the insulated or splintered truth of an epigram, which leads him sometimes to extend the laws or definition of rhetoric and sometimes to admit its inferiority unless complemented by eloquence. There can be no truth-telling, he says, unless the feelings are involved; for without 'spontaneous feelings' truth must rest upon 'artificial aids'. De Quincey's skill in making subtle distinctions and his attention to Wordsworth for once desert him. His attempt to re-establish rhetoric as a fine art is a surprising shift from everything he had learned from Wordsworth; but Wordsworth had no time for so simple a distinction between the feelings and 'artificial aids':

> Substitute for the word 'artificially' the word 'artfully' and you will at once see that nothing can be more erroneous than the assertion. The word 'artificially' begs the question, because that word is always employed in an unfavourable sense.[15]

De Quincey is more convincing when he suggests that rhetoric at its finest tends towards eloquence; less convincing when he claims (a confusing notion) that the greatest literature combines the two. Sir Walter Raleigh had 'a great original capacity' for rhetoric; but the finest passages of his prose 'are touched with a sadness too pathetic and of too personal a growth, to fulfil the conditions' of rhetoric. And though Bacon (as we saw) was too much in search of absolute truth to play the game of rhetoric, he could well have been a great rhetorician since he had 'no feelings too profound, or of a nature to disturb the balance of a pleasurable activity'. One by one De Quincey's great English rhetoricians are shown to be something more; and their greatness depends on that something. English rhetoric prospered, he says, from the end of the sixteenth to the middle of the seventeenth century;

> and, though the English Rhetoric was less rigorously true to its own ideal than the Roman, and often modulated into a

higher key of impassioned eloquence, yet unquestionably in some of its qualities it remains a monument of the very finest rhetorical powers. (Masson, X, 100)

It is feeling, of course, which distinguishes eloquence from rhetoric; yet it is this eloquence which enables Taylor to display 'the very finest rhetorical powers'. The word 'impassioned' describes the distinguishing (and distinguished) quality of eloquence. John Donne is the first 'very eminent rhetorician' in English literature. Dr. Johnson was wrong to call him a metaphysical poet; '*Rhetorical* would have been a more accurate designation.' In his verse and in his prose he combined rhetoric's 'dialectical subtlety and address' with 'the most impassioned majesty'. In a passage from Sir Thomas Browne's *Urn-Burial* De Quincey finds an 'impassioned requiem' and also a '*fluctus decumanus*' of rhetoric. In Jeremy Taylor there is 'the everlasting strife and fluctuation between his rhetoric and his eloquence'. The opulence of his rhetoric is apt to be 'oppressive', but this tendency was 'checked and balanced' by the 'commanding passion' and 'intensity' of his theme which 'gave a final unity to the tumultuous motions of his intellect'. In *Paradise Regained* the oratory of Satan in the Wilderness is no longer rhetoric, but 'in the grandest style of impassioned eloquence'. Even Burke was only seldom a pure rhetorician 'consciously and profusely lavishing his ornaments for mere purpose effect'. He was 'the man of the largest and finest understanding. Upon that word, *understanding*, we lay a stress' in order to contrast it with the too common view of Burke's writings as the product of fancy. 'Fancy in your throats, ye miserable twaddlers! As if Edmund Burke were the man to play with his fancy for the purpose of separable ornament.' Burke, says De Quincey, using italics to make the important point, 'does not as a rule *dress* his thoughts in imagery but *incarnates* them'. In Burke, as in the great seventeenth-century prose-writers, the feeling or passion of their writings transmutes their rhetoric into eloquence; and eloquence turns out to be (in part through its incarnate imagery) the literature of power. 'Without sentiment, without imagery,' asks De Quincey, 'how should it be possible for rhetoric to subsist?' And conversely, where there are 'strains of feeling, genuine or not, supported at every step from the excitement of independent objects', there can be no rhetoric. Sometimes De Quincey's distinctions multiply; from the strife and fluctuation and mighty opposition of rhetoric and eloquence of Jeremy Taylor and Sir Thomas Browne, can emerge something greater than either:

> In them . . . are the two opposite forces of eloquent passion and rhetorical fancy brought into an exquisite equilibrium, – approaching, receding, – attracting, repelling, – blending, separating, – chasing and chased, as in a fugue, – and again lost in a delightful interfusion, so as to create a middle species of composition, more various and stimulating to the understanding than pure eloquence, more gratifying to the affections than naked rhetoric. (Masson, X, 104–5)

But the critical equipoise is not maintained. Sir Thomas Browne requires no 'bravura' or 'antiphon' to his 'sublime rapture'. Jeremy Taylor has something of Shakespeare's 'myriad-mindedness' and like him he does not unfold, but creates. In the end he sounds like a seventeenth-century Wordsworth, as De Quincey finds in his work 'old thoughts surveyed from novel stations and under various angles', and 'a sense of novelty diffused over truths coeval with human life'.[16]

5 The Art of Prose

'To walk well, it is not enough that a man abstains from dancing.'

I

In the 'General Preface' of 1853 to James Hogg's Edinburgh edition of his collected works, De Quincey drew attention to the variety of his prose and to the originality of his prose-poems or impassioned prose. He made three divisions of what he had written; the largest section of his work was made up of what he called 'essays', which he defined as writings 'which address themselves to the understanding as an insulated faculty'. Essays present a problem and try to solve it, and the only questions to be asked are 'what is the success obtained?' and (as a separate question) 'What is the executive ability displayed in the solution of the problem?' Even today nearly all these essays are entertaining, informative and lively; but there was nothing new in De Quincy's way of treating such external subjects, and the only originality is to be found in De Quincey's use of paradox for polemical purposes. The second division of his work consisted of what he called 'Autobiographic Sketches', and for these he claimed little 'beyond that sort of amusement which attaches to any real story, thoughtfully and faithfully related'. At times, however, the narrative rose 'into a far higher key'; for these moments he asked from the reader 'a higher consideration', and, in fact, they occurred when the narrative ceased for a while; when no story carried the reader forward, when nothing of external interest could appeal to him, when simply there was 'nothing on the stage but a solitary infant, and its solitary combat with grief – a mighty darkness, and a sorrow without a voice'. Such moments, claims De Quincey, have far more than mere amusement to offer; in them he has tried 'to see and measure these mystical forces which palsy him', and has attempted 'to pierce the haze which so often envelops, even to himself, his own secret springs of action and reserve'. Such passages are scarcely to be distinguished (another example in De Quincey of distinction without difference?) from the third division of his prose; 'a far higher class of compositions' in which he ranks the *Confessions* 'and also (but more emphatically) the *Suspiria de Profundis'*. And here De Quincey lays claim to originality; both works are 'modes of impassioned prose ranging under no precedents that I am aware of in any literature'. The only confessions of the past that have interested men are those of St. Augustine and Rousseau. 'The very idea of breathing a record of human passion ... argues an impassioned theme' and 'impassioned, therefore, should be the tenor of the composition'. But in St. Augustine's *Confessions* there is only one 'impassioned passage' (on the death of his young friend in the fourth Book); in Rousseau's *Confessions* 'there is not even so much. In the whole work there is nothing grandly affecting but the character and the inexplicable misery of the writer.'[1]

De Quincey makes 'haughtier pretensions' for originality in the conception of these writings than for their execution; but the new areas of experience which he explored could not be separated from the prose which revealed them. No one, indeed, insisted more than De Quincey that 'manner blends inseparably with substance' and that matter and style, mind and style, even character and style, were indissolubly bonded or, to use one of his own favourite words, 'coadunated'. 'Were a magnificent dedication required,' he writes, 'were a *Defensio pro Populo Anglicano* required, Southey's is not the mind, and, by a necessary consequence, Southey's is not the style, for carrying such purposes into full and memorable effect.' Style, he claims elsewhere, is an indirect expression of a writer's 'nature and moral feelings'. The prevailing tone of Charles Lamb's style 'was in part influenced (or at least sustained) by his disgust for all which transcended the naked simplicity of truth'. Above all, in any writing where the thoughts are subjective, 'in that same proportion does the very essence become identical with the expression, and the style become confluent with the matter'.[2]

Even as a child De Quincey had been aware of how difficult it was in the ordinary language of men to communicate, for example, his 'solitary combat with grief':

> My mother was predisposed to think ill of all causes that required many words: I, predisposed to subtleties of all sorts and degrees, had naturally become acquainted with cases that could not unrobe their apparellings down to that degree of simplicity. If in this world there is one misery having no relief, it is the pressure on the heart from the *Incommunicable*. And, if another Sphinx should arise to propose another enigma to man – saying, What burden is that which only is insupportable by human fortitude? I should answer at once – *It is the burden of the Incommunicable*. (Masson, III, 315)

At that time nothing which offered itself to his rhetoric 'gave any but the feeblest and most childish reflection of my past sufferings'. Later his impassioned prose would communicate all that he now found incommunicable; not simply the sufferings of childhood, but its dreams, sudden intuitions, forebodings, its inexplicable sorrows and sudden memories, its half hints of connections between past and present and future. De Quincey makes it clear that his 'dreaming tendencies' were 'constitutional and not dependent on laudanum'. When he tells of his childhood dreams of 'terrific grandeur' it is because he believes that 'psychological experiences of deep suffering or joy first attain their entire fulness of expression when they are reverberated from dreams'.[3]

De Quincey's dreams, and the word includes waking visionary moments, are the best known things about his childhood, but he communicated more than these. Two incidents in his life before he reached his second birthday left 'stings in my memory so as to be remembered at this day'; that is, sixty years later. One was, indeed, a remarkable dream; but the other was 'the fact of having connected a profound sense of pathos with the reappearance very early in the spring of some crocuses'. Childhood, says De Quincey, enjoys 'a limited privilege of strength':

> The heart in this season of life is apprehensive; and where its sensibilities are profound, is endowed with a special

power of listening for the tones of truth – hidden, struggling or remote. (Masson, I, 121–2)

Infancy is a separate and distinct period of a man's life, but it is also 'part of a larger world that waits for its final comple-ment in old age'. In the second chapter of his *Autobiography*, 'The Affliction of Childhood', he tells of the death of his much loved elder sister Elizabeth at the age of nine, when De Quin-cey himself was six years old; but the chapter has a prelimi-nary paragraph before he begins to describe his sister and his deep love for her:

> About the close of my sixth year, suddenly the first chapter of my life came to a violent termination; that chapter which, even within the gates of recovered Paradise, might merit a remembrance. *'Life is Finished!'* was the secret misgiving of my heart; for the heart of infancy is as apprehensive as that of maturest wisdom in relation to any capital wound inflicted on the happiness. *'Life is Finished! Finished it is!'* was the hidden meaning that, half-unconsciously to myself, lurked within my sighs; and, as bells heard from a distance on a summer evening seem charged at times with an articu-late form of words, some monitory message, that rolls round unceasingly, even so for me some noiseless and subterrane-ous voice seemed to chant continually a secret word, made audible only to my own heart – that 'now is the blossoming of life withered for ever'. Not that such words formed them-selves vocally within my ear, or issued audibly from my lips: but such a whisper stole silently to my heart. (Masson, I, 28)

The chapter ends with two short passages entitled 'Dream-Echoes of these Infant Experiences' and 'Dream-Echoes Fifty Years Later'; the afflictions of childhood becomes the afflic-tions of manhood. The first passage describes an episode twelve years after the death of his sister, when De Quincey was at Oxford and had tasted opium and experienced the extra power of opium dreams: 'And now first the agitation of my childhood reopened in strength; now first they swept in upon the brain with power and the grandeur of recovered life'[4]

> So feeling comes in aid
> Of feeling, and diversity of strength
> Attend us, if but once we have been strong.

In the second passage he refers to 'the transfigurings worked upon troubled remembrances by retrospects so vast as those of fifty years'.

To describe the hidden meanings that half-consciously lurked within his sighs, or explain the pathos of the crocuses, or describe 'the tones of truth' and the eruptions of memory and the transfigurings wrought by dreams upon the apprehensions and scarcely understood experiences of childhood, needed a very different kind of prose that could accommodate 'subtleties of all sorts and degrees'; a prose which by the very nature of the subject could not (as his mother wished) be brief or be expressive in a small compass. One of many extended musical metaphors describes what De Quincey wished to do in prose, and shows him doing it:

A song, an air, a tune, – that is, a short succession of notes revolving rapidly upon itself, – how could that, by possibility, offer a field of compass sufficient for the development of great musical effects! The preparation pregnant with the future; the remote correspondence; the questions, as it were, which to a deep musical sense are asked in one passage and answered in another; the iteration and ingemination of a given effect, moving through subtle variations that sometimes disguise the theme, sometimes fitfully reveal it, sometimes throw it out tumultuously to the blaze of daylight: these and ten thousand forms of self-conflicting musical passion, – what room could they find, what opening, what utterance, in so limited a field as an air or song? (Masson, X, 136)

A 'remote correspondence' or the 'ingemination of a given effect' could not be achieved either by an automatically antithetic prose where in no sentence is there 'any dependency on what goes before', or by the 'lifeless mechanism' of eighteenth-century prose. Dr. Johnson's prose never 'GROWS a truth before your eyes whilst in the act of delivering it. His prose offers no process, no evolution, no movement of self-conflict or preparation'; only distinctions, 'a definite outline of limitation', antitheses and the dissipating of some 'casual perplexity'.[5] The capitalised 'GROWS' suggests that De Quincey will need to create a prose that is (he uses the word) organic and exploratory.

De Quincey needed first of all to insist that prose was an art and the equal of poetry. There had been great prose-writers in the past, but on the subject of prose style De Quincey had found 'nothing of any value in modern writers' and 'not much as regards the grounds and ultimate principles' in the Greek and Roman rhetoricians. For too long readers and critics had assumed that there could never be rules or a theory of prose since prose was considered to be merely 'the negation of verse'; and that to be a writer of prose meant only 'the privilege of being inartificial', and a dispensation from 'the restraints of metre'.

> But this is ignorance, though a pretty common ignorance. To walk well, it is not enough that a man abstains from dancing. Walking has rules of its own the more difficult to perceive or to practise as they are less broadly *prononcés*. To forbear singing is not, therefore, to speak well or to read well: each of which offices rests upon a separate art of its own. Numerous laws of transition, connexion, preparation, are different for a writer in verse and a writer in prose. Each mode of composition is a great art; well executed, is the highest and most difficult of arts. (Masson, VI, 100)

It is the fluency and plasticity of prose, its slow preparation of great effects, its ability to follow the subtlest contours of experience, its power to be 'dark with Cassandra meanings', which De Quincey wants to establish. To achieve these ends the writer will have to observe 'the two capital secrets in the art of prose composition'. The first of these is 'the philosophy of transition and connection, or the art by which one step in an evolution of thought is made to arise out of another: all fluent and effective composition depends on the *connections*'.

The second follows from this and is 'the way in which sentences are made to modify each other; for the most powerful effects in written eloquence arise out of this reverberation'. No sentence must be an independent whole. And length of sentence is no security, for 'German prose tends to such immoderate length of sentences that no effect of intermodification can ever be apparent': the Germans have 'no eloquence'.[6] The art of prose is the art of being eloquent. Eloquence is poetry and power; it is the literature of powerfully moved feelings of any sort. The art of prose depends on that art of 'connexions' (De Quincey never tires of the word) which will recreate for the reader the unity imposed by dreams or memory on the randomness of experience.

Most of what De Quincey has to say about prose-style or the art of prose is description of his own impassioned prose or the eloquent prose of other writers. He is so anxious to insist on the hidden capacities of prose, its ability as great as poetry's to describe the most complex feelings and to move the reader, that he can sometimes seem to reject all other kinds of prose; 'for, unless on a question which admits some action of the feelings', he claims that 'style, properly defined, is impossible'. All prose, says De Quincey, must be judged by its appropriateness, and therefore its effectiveness. In the house of prose there are many mansions; some are bigger and more beautiful than others, but all are fit and useful for some purpose. Addison has an apt grace in a certain line of composition, 'but it is only one line among many, and it is far from being among the highest'.

Governing everything De Quincey says about prose is the traditional notion of decorum. No prose style is 'absolutely good – good unconditionally, no matter what the subject'. For too long readers have assumed that a simple prose was the best prose and was adequate for any subject; Swift, Defoe and Addison are therefore selected as models. But simple, good prose of this kind was very common in the eighteenth century. The fact that hundreds of religious writers managed effective simple prose should surprise no one, since all that the subject required was 'plain good sense, natural feeling, unpretendingness' and some skill in 'putting together the clockwork of sentences'. Their subject rightly rejected all ornament. 'All depends upon the subject.' The 'unelevated and *unrhythmical*' style of Addison or Swift can manage many things; the prose of *Gulliver's Travels*, for example, is '*purposely* touched slightly with that dulness of circumstantiality which besets the excellent, but somewhat dull, race of men, – old sea-captains'. But 'grand impassioned subjects insist upon a different treatment; and there it is that the true difficulties of style commence', and there it is that 'Master Jonathan would have broke down irrecoverably'.[7] The simple style is right for simple things;

> [but] there is a style transcending these and all other modes of simplicity by infinite degrees, and in the same proportion impossible to most men: the rhythmical – the continuous – what in French is called the *soutenu*; which to humbler styles stands in the relation of an organ to a shepherd's pipe. This also finds its justification in its subject; and the subject which *can* justify it must be of a corresponding quality – loftier, and, therefore, rare. (Masson, III, 51)

Everything is subject to the laws of decorum; but a writer of any talent and sense will consciously and inevitably obey such laws, because (style and subject being one) having 'no grand impassioned subject' he could neither wish nor need nor be able to deal with such a subject. Southey's mind, for example, was 'not sustained by the higher modes of enthusiasm', and therefore he had not the style to plead passionately against oppression. 'His style is *therefore* good, because it has been suited to his themes,' and his themes were not of a kind 'to allow a thought of eloquence, or of the periodic style which a perfect eloquence instinctively seeks'. The direct style of Charles James Fox is good and is justified by its subject; he was 'simple in his manners, simple in his style, simple in his thought'. Addison was incapable of 'impassioned grandeur' and of 'any expression of sympathy with the lovely, the noble, or the impassioned.[8] In every case De Quincey finds that the limits of the writer's style are the limits of his world.

II

But De Quincey had new and larger worlds to explore and conquer. His own experiences and dreams in childhood, his deep, deep memories and the later pains of his opium dreams had convinced him of the 'one uninterrupted bond of unity running through the entire succession of experiences, first and last'; his profoundest conviction was of 'the dark sympathy, which runs underground, connecting remote events like a ground-swell in the ocean'; and his wish was to reveal in his prose the else 'undiscoverable web of dependency of one thing on another'.[9] This conviction of remote correspondences, of 'filaments fine but inseverable' which gave a unity and coherence where to the eye of vulgar logic none existed, showed itself in many other ways than in his own impassioned prose. It led him, appropriately, to a richly sympathetic account of Coleridge's conversation. What most impressed De Quincey was the way in which Coleridge could traverse 'the most spacious fields of thought by transitions the most just and logical':

> What I mean by saying that his transitions were 'just' is by way of contradistinction to that mode of conversation which courts variety through links of *verbal* connexions. Coleridge, to many people . . . seemed to wander; and he seemed then to wander the most when, in fact, his resistance to the wandering instinct was greatest – viz., when the compass and huge circuit by which his illustrations moved travelled farthest into remote regions before they began to revolve. Long before this coming round commenced most people had lost him, and naturally enough supposed that he had lost himself. They continued to admire the separate beauty of the thoughts, but did not see their relations to the dominant theme. (Masson, II, 152–3)

What De Quincey admires here is that poetic logic which Coleridge had said was 'as severe as that of science; and more difficult, because more subtle, more complex, and dependent on more and more fugitive causes'.[10] De Quincey, using the word as Coleridge had used it, declared that he had 'a logical instinct for feeling in a moment the secret analogies or parallelisms that connected things else apparently remote'; and in his autobiography said that he neglected 'harsher logic', and connected the separate sections of his sketches 'not by ropes and cables, but by threads of aerial gossamer'. The same concern for connections, for the 'filaments' which create unity, explains his reluctance to comment much on individual lines of verse; a certain line is 'not a good line *when insulated*' but is better 'in its connexion with the entire succession of which it forms part'.[11] And the same passion for the unity born of connections explains De Quincey's surprising enthusiasm for Ricardo and political economy; 'it is eminently an organic science' for every part 'acts on the whole as the whole again reacts on and through each part'.[12]

De Quincey, then, wished to explore new worlds of experience and needed a new prose for the purpose. He had found no help, he said, in either modern writers on prose or in the ancient rhetoricians, and was therefore obliged 'to collect my opinions from the great artists and practitioners' rather than from the theorists. He found the examples he needed in three places: in Greek prose-writers, especially Herodotus and Demosthenes; in some English seventeenth-century writers such as Sir Thomas Browne and Jeremy Taylor; and in Burke.

Herodotus and Demosthenes had one great advantage: they wrote in Greek; and

> the Greek is, beyond comparison, the most plastic of languages. It was a material which bent to the purposes of him who used it beyond the material of other languages; it was an instrument for a larger compass of modulations; and it happens that the peculiar theme of an orator imposes the very largest which is consistent with a prose diction. One step further in passion, and the orator would become a poet. (Masson, III, 63–4)

De Quincey believed that in his own prose he had, indeed, taken that 'one step further in passion'; he wanted above all to make English prose 'an instrument for a larger compass of modulations', a language 'plastic' enough to follow the very contours of his own subtle, complex, barely communicable experiences.

Herodotus was his favourite. De Quincey seems to be thinking of his own digressive method in dozens of magazine articles and biographical sketches when he says of Herodotus that

he was 'a writer whose works do actually, in their major proportion, not essentially concern that subject to which by their
translated title they are exclusively referred; or even that part
which *is* historical often moves by mere anecdotes or personal
sketches'.[13] But, of course, De Quincey sees Herodotus as the
'Father of Prose', as 'the leader of prose composition'. 'And if
it is objected that Herodotus was *not* the eldest of prose writers, doubtless, in an absolute sense, no man was.' But
'Herodotus was to prose composition what Homer, six
hundred years earlier, had been to Verse'. He was 'a great
liberal artist' in prose, 'an *intellectual* potentate'[14] who established prose as an art with separate laws of its own, 'laws of
transition, connexion, preparation'. Herodotus was a *power* in
literature. Isocrates is condemned; his style is not organic; he
'cultivated the *rhythmus* of his periods' and to this end sacrificed 'the freedom and natural movement of his thoughts'.
Demosthenes, in spite of his many gifts, rarely pursued a
theme with 'the requisite fulness of development or illustration'. His faults can be blamed on his audience who, 'being
always on the fret, – kept the orator on the fret'. He could not,
dared not, be eloquent; 'hence arose short sentences; hence
the impossibility of the long, voluminous sweeps of beautiful
rhythmus'. His style is spirited and animated but not full of
'continuous grandeur'. He had to keep 'the *immediate* – the
instant' before his eye and could not quit 'the direct path of
the question' even for any purpose of 'ultimate effect'.

'Continuous grandeur' was to be found in certain prose
writers of the seventeenth century. De Quincey found that
'Donne, Chillingworth, Sir Thomas Browne, Jeremy Taylor,
Milton, South, Barrow form a *pleïad*, a constellation of seven
golden stars such as no literature can match in their own
class'. They provide the 'highest efforts of eloquence in all
English literature'.[15] It is not simply the grandeur or musical-
ity of their prose which appeals to De Quincey, but its continuity. The innumerable musical images which he uses to
describe its effect are not attempts to praise the mere sound
and sonority of seventeenth-century periods, but to suggest
the complex, organic, musical structure which organises separate items into a rich unity. Every single separate sentence is,
indeed, 'a subject for complex art'; but 'it is in the *relation* of

sentences that the true life of composition resides'. Sentences, he says, must have 'logic and sensuous qualities – rhythm, for instance, or the continuity of metaphor';[16] as a piece of music has a theme which recurs in a dozen different ways enriched, elaborated, extended, disguised, but through it all 'lurks to the last'. De Quincey argued that very often, and especially when the matter is the very feelings of the writer, the manner *is* the matter. His own matter was very often the continuity of experience, the slow preparation of effects, the transubstantiation through memory of childhood incidents, the revelation of connections. Seventeenth-century prose provided examples of the art of preparation and connections; of an eloquence which 'prolongs itself, repeats itself, propagates itself'. Jeremy Taylor's prose is 'all alive with the subtlety of distinctions'; but this is happily matched and balanced by 'the commanding passion and intensity' of his theme, which gives 'a final unity to the tumultuous motions of his intellect'.

> *Human life*, for example, *is short*; *human happiness is frail*; how trite, how obvious a thesis? Yet, in the beginning of the *Holy Dying*, upon that simplest of themes how magnificent a descant! Variations the most original upon a ground the most universal . . . (Masson, X, 125)

Where but in Sir Thomas Browne, exclaims De Quincey, is it possible to find 'music so Miltonic, an intonation of such solemn chords' as are struck in *Urn-Burial*; but these chords are simply the beginning of 'a melodious ascent as of a prelude to some impassioned requiem'.[17]

Burke had much in common with these earlier prose-writers, but was an even more congenial revelation of the resources of prose since he moved 'among moving things and uncertainties, as compared with the more stationary aspects of moral philosophy'. In his writings there is process, evolution, preparation, and always some 'oblique glance' at 'remote affinities'. At the very moment of writing, 'every truth, be it what it may, every thesis of a sentence, *grows* in the very act of unfolding it'. Whatever he begins with receives 'a new determination or inflexion at every clause'. His prose is perpetually creative; and, as with Jeremy Taylor, the connections, coherence and unity of his writing are provided by continuity of metaphor. In both writers 'the fancy' (by which De Quincey means the imagination) 'is the express organ of the judgment'. In some writers the metaphors are 'mere embellishments':

> Now, on the contrary, in Taylor and Burke, everything figurative is part and parcel of the process of thinking, and incarnated with the thought; it is not a separate descant *on* what they think, but a part of the organ, by which they think . . . no passage can be produced from either of them, in which the imagery does no more than repeat and reflect the naked unillustrated thought, but that there is some latent feature, or relation of the truth revealed by the imagery, which could not have been revealed without it.

Burke was 'overmastered by the weight of the truth he was communicating'; and so it was 'the necessity of his understanding, dealing with subtle truths, that required a perpetual light of analogy, (the *idem in altero*) for making them apprehensible'.[18]

Not all prose-writers of the seventeenth century merit the same praise as De Quincey gives to his *pleïad*. Bacon suffers from 'the shorthand style of his composition, in which the connexions are seldom fully developed'. Burton is too 'disjointed'; he is 'not so much fanciful as capricious; his motion is not the motion of freedom, but of lawlessness; he does not dance but caper'.[19] For De Quincey, who insists strongly that a writer's mind and style are inseparable, a 'disjointed' style would make it impossible for him to communicate his sense of the connectedness of things, his instinct for secret analogies. A disjointed or simple style can communicate only disjointed or simple things. De Quincey himself is seldom (in the modern sense of the word) a witty writer; a book that is 'aphoristic', he says, is a book 'without a plan'. (He applies the same criticism to long poems. Pope's *Essay on Criticism* is 'a collection of independent maxims . . . having no natural order or logical dependence', and therefore no power of connections in the thought.) A simple style, 'the *style coupé* as opposed to the *style soutenu*' prefers 'the subsultory to the continuous' and therefore cannot explore the subtleties of a subject.

> In order to be brief a man must take a short sweep of view; his range of thought cannot be extensive; and such a rule, applied to a general method of thinking, is fitted rather to aphorisms and maxims, as upon a known subject, than to any process of investigation as upon a subject yet to be fathomed. (Masson, X, 166)

Fox's style was simple because there were 'no waters in *him* turbid with new crystallizations; everywhere the eye could see to the bottom'.[20] The 'general terseness' of Junius and his short sentences would have been impossible if he had been forced into 'a wider compass of thought' or into a 'higher subject'. The simplicity and clarity of maxim or aphorism are easy 'where new growths are not germinating', but they can be purchased at too high a rate. Without that elaborate prose which is necessary to growth and full expression, 'much truth and beauty must perish in germ'. (Bacon, says De Quiney, was merely an acorn; Jeremy Taylor was an oak.) Its music may, indeed, be 'dark with Cassandra meaning'; but 'who complains of a prophet for being a little darker in speech than a post-office directory'.[21]

It is not only written prose that De Quincey considers, but the prose of conversation. In 'the velocities and contagious ardour' of conversation, there was likely to be even less distinction between a man's mind and interests and their necessary reflection in his language. Conversation, too, was an art; but by conversation De Quincey means something closer to the Platonic dialectic than the negative energy (as he saw it) of even so mighty a talker as Dr. Johnson. And conversation could make creative thinking perhaps more possible than written prose; it was certainly congenial to De Quincey and his purpose:

> I felt (and in this I could not be mistaken, as too certainly it was a fact of my own experience) that in the electric kindling of life between two minds . . . there sometimes arise glimpses and shy revelations of affinity, suggestion, relation, analogy, that could not have been approached through any avenues of methodical study.

And again he used his favourite musical imagery:

> Great organists find the same effect of inspiration, the same result of power creative and revealing, in the mere movement and velocity of their own voluntaries ... these *impromptu* torrents of music create rapturous *fioriture*, beyond all capacity in the artist to register, or afterwards to imitate. (Masson, X, 268–9)

De Quincey praises the best conversation for being organic, for being an example of what he calls 'organology'. The great (though rare) gift of conversation, and the reason why he valued it, was that in it 'approximations are more obvious and easily effected between things too remote for a steadier contemplation'. I have already quoted De Quincey's description of Coleridge's conversation; elsewhere he writes that the distinguishing feature of his talk was its 'power of vast combination': he 'gathered into focal concentration the largest body of objects *apparently* disconnected'.[22] On the other hand Southey's 'epigrammatic form of delivering opinions has a certain effect of *clenching* a subject'; it is 'the style of his mind' which leads him to adapt 'a trenchant, pungent, aculeated form of terse, glittering, stenographic sentences', ending with a 'contentious aphorism' which informs the reader that 'the record is closed'.[23]

A description by Thomas Hood of De Quincey's own talk makes him sound like Coleridge and shows how close for De Quincey the connection was between writing and talking:

> I have found him at home, quite at home in the midst of a German Ocean of literature, in a storm, flooding all the floor, the table and the chairs – billows of books, tossing, tumbling, surging open – on such occasions I have willingly listened by the hour, whilst the philosopher, standing with his eyes fixed on one side of the room, seemed to be less speaking than reading from 'a handwriting on the wall'. Now and then he would diverge for a Scotch mile or two, to the right or left ... but he always came safely back to the point where he had left, not lost the scent, and thence hunted his topic to the end.[24]

Disjointed, discontinuous, aphoristic prose or talk was not suitable for noting the 'links uniting remote incidents which else seemed casual and disconnected'; a simple prose would not wait for De Quincey's truths to unfold themselves. It could not treat of a moment in childhood that 'reproduces itself in some future perplexity' and which years later would 'come back in some reversionary shape'. It could not show how the child was father of the man, or follow the movement of dreams or the eruptions of memory through involutes, 'the almost infinite intricacy of their movements'. And again De Quincey uses the analogy of music to describe the 'organic' prose which his subjects demanded:

> A curve is long in showing its elements of fluxion; we must watch long in order to compute them; we must wait in order to know the law of their relations and the music of the deep mathematical principles which they obey. A piece of music, again, from the great hand of Mozart or Beethoven, which seems a mere anarchy to the dull, material mind, to the ear which is instructed by a deep sensibility reveals a law of controlling power, determining its movements, its actions and reactions, such as cannot be altogether hidden, even when as yet it is but dimly perceived.[25]

De Quincey's search is always for the law that explains and gives coherence to the richness and seeming randomness of separate experiences and 'connects the scattered phenomena into their rigorous unity'.

Nothing can be creatively understood in a limited prose. When De Quincey comments on prose-writers he finds that the inadequacy of their prose reflects the limits of their imaginative intelligence. It is in comments on Lamb and Hazlitt that De Quincey makes most clear his belief in the inseparability of manner and matter in prose, and in the capacity and resourcefulness of prose to do what his great contemporaries were doing in verse. Hazlitt was neither an eloquent writer nor a comprehensive thinker, and his failures could be seen in his prose:

Hazlitt was not eloquent, because he was discontinuous. No

man can be eloquent whose thoughts are abrupt, insulated, capricious, and (to borrow an impressive word from Coleridge) non-sequacious. Eloquence resides not in separate or fractional ideas, but in the relations of manifold ideas, and in the mode of their evolution from each other. It is not indeed enough that the ideas should be many, and their relations coherent; the main condition lies in the *key* of the evolution, in the *law* of the succession. The elements are nothing without the atmosphere that moulds, and the dynamic forces that combine. (Masson, V, 231)

All De Quincey's favourite pejorative adjectives are here and all his favourite terms of praise; and the reference to Coleridge reminds us of the very different subjects and different prose which De Quincey has in mind. The '*key* of the evolution' and 'the *law* of the succession' are the necessary subtle logic of poetry which Coleridge discovered from his schoolmaster at Christ's Hospital and which is the necessary condition of all eloquent writing in verse or prose. De Quincey wants a prose that 'moulds' and 'combines' all the fragments into a unity. Subtle truths require 'a perpetual light of analogy'; but Hazlitt does not provide the continuity of metaphor which might provide this light, since 'his brilliancy is seen chiefly in separate splinterings of phrase or image' which 'spread no deep suffusions of colour'. It could not be otherwise, because his thoughts 'were of the same fractured and discontinuous order as his illustrative images – seldom or never self-diffusive'. Hazlitt had no principles upon any subject. He viewed all things 'under the angle which chance circumstances presented, never from a central station'; he was at the mercy of every random impulse, and so his 'eternal paradoxes' have not even 'a momentary consistency amongst each other', but are always 'shifting, collapsing, moulding and unmoulding themselves like the dancing pillars of sand of the deserts'.[26] Lamb, it is true, did not agree with de Quincey's comments on Hazlitt; but, then, Lamb's prose suffered in the same way. His mind, like Hazlitt's in its 'movement and style of feeling', was 'discontinuous and abrupt'. He necessarily confined himself to 'short flights' since his own 'constitution of intellect sinned by this very habit of discontinuity'. He shrank from 'the continuous, from the sustained, from the elaborate'; when he writes, his sentiment does not 'propagate itself'. De Quincey finds that other features of Lamb's mind would have argued this weakness in his prose by analogy; he was totally insensible to music, to the complex structure of music and therefore of prose composition.

'The English Mail-Coach'[27] is an example of the new areas of experience which De Quincey made fit subjects for prose, and of the prose 'without precedent in any literature' that could encompass and express them. The article, in two parts, had originally appeared in *Blackwood's Magazine* in 1849, four years after the *Suspiria de Profundis* with which it naturally belongs. When De Quincey prepared the article for the Collective Edition of his writings in 1854 he divided it into its present three sections and De Quincey's editor notes that 'great care was bestowed in the revision. Passages that had appeared in the magazine articles were omitted; new sentences were inserted; and the language was retouched throughout'.[28] In spite of this care, De Quincey mentions in a 'Postscript' added in 1854 (but not usually included in modern editions) that not all readers had understood the article:

> To my surprise, however, one or two critics, not carelessly in conversation, but deliberately in print, professed their inability to apprehend the meaning of the whole, or to follow the links of the connexion between its several parts. I am myself as little able to understand where the difficulty lies, or to detect any lurking obscurity, as these critics found themselves to unravel my logic. (Masson, XIII, 328)

He then goes on to make clear the 'logic' and 'links of connexion' which will establish (to use phrases from elsewhere in his work) 'the close convergence of the several parts' and will demonstrate how the whole essay is 'a coherent work of art'.

The three sections of 'The English Mail-Coach' are 'The Glory of Motion', 'The Vision of Sudden Death' and 'Dream-Fugue', to which De Quincey appended the explanatory sub-title, 'Founded on the Preceding Theme of Sudden Death'. The several titles hint already at the 'logic' and 'connexions' of the parts; the words 'glory', 'vision' and 'dream' make clear that De Quincey is dealing with heightened states of awareness. (Wordsworth in 'Strange Fits of Passion' had dared to tell his story only in 'the Lover's ear' who alone would understand the interconnections and associations of things under the influence of deep feeling.) He explains that the whole paper had its origin in the second section, 'The Vision of Sudden Death':

> Thirty-seven years ago, or rather more, accident made me, in the dead of night, and of a night memorably solemn, the solitary witness of an appalling scene, which threatened instant death in a shape the most terrific to two young people whom I had no means of assisting, except in so far as I was able to give them a most hurried warning of their danger; but even *that* not until they stood within the very shadow of catastrophe, being divided from the most frightful of deaths by scarcely more, if more at all, than seventy seconds. (Masson, XIII, 328–9)

From this scene, he says, 'the whole of this paper radiates as a natural expansion'; and in the two final pages of 'The Vision of Sudden Death' De Quincey makes clear how and why this radiating will occur.

De Quincey had been helpless to avert the threatening collison of the two coaches and when it happened he was sure that the woman had been killed. As the coaches collided and then separated he looked back on the scene which 'wrote all its records on my heart for ever'. A few lines later he is sure that the sight of the woman throwing her arms 'wildly to heaven will never depart from my dreams'; in the closing lines of the section a curve in the road removed the scene from his eyes and 'swept it into my dreams for ever'. In his 'Postscript' De Quincey adds that it was swept into 'a rolling succession of dreams, each one as tumultuous and changing as a musical fugue'. It is natural, therefore, that the final section should recount these dreams or nightmares.

If this had been all, every reader could have unravelled the logic and followed the thread of transition and connection; for in his dreams all the 'elements of the scene blended, under the law of association'. But there were other elements in the

dream which readers failed to understand because by no
associations could they be connected with 'The Vision of Sudden Death': 'Waterloo, I understand, was the particular feature of the "Dream-Fugue" which my censors were least able
to account for'. The explanation does not lie, as De Quincey
might have pleaded, in the thought that for thousands of men
Waterloo offered visions of sudden and violent death: De
Quincey's law of association is tauter and its logic more subtle
than this. It is found in that phrase in the 'Postscript' where
he says that it was from the second section that 'the whole of
this paper radiates as a natural expansion'. The 'whole' of his
paper includes the relaxed, even chatty, first section in which
De Quincey explains that it was via the regular mail-coach
services from London that news of great national victories
such as Waterloo was carried to the provinces. His imagination had already been seized by this in the first section: 'The
mail-coach it was that distributed over the face of the land,
like the opening of apocalyptic vials, the heart-shaking news
of Trafalgar, of Salamanca, of Vittoria, of Waterloo.' Such
excited imaginings had already done something to heighten
the state of consciousness which, in the second section, the
beauty of the night and dawn and the sudden threatening
danger raised still further.

The general title of the article, 'The English Mail-Coach', is
an accurate one; the elements in the dreams are to be traced
back to happenings and feelings in section one which preceded
by at least several hours the vision and near disaster of the
second section. Even on the very first page of the opening
section De Quincey had already hinted at how the article
would end:

> But, finally, that particular element in this whole combina-
> tion which most impressed myself, and through which it is
> that to this hour Mr. Palmer's mail-coach system tyrannises
> over my dreams by terror and terrific beauty, lay in the
> awful political mission which at that time it fulfilled. (Mas-
> son, XIII, 272)

The disparate elements in the first two sections are picked up
again in the 'Dream-Fugue', and, in De Quincey's excellent

phrase, 'the whole is gathered into unity by a reflex act of meditation'.

De Quincey explains two other apocalyptic elements in his dreams, two other examples of separate experiences which, when recurring in dreams, became 'symbolically significant'. In his dreams the mail-coach galloped through a vast cathedral; and a sculpture of a dying trumpeter suddenly rose to his feet and 'unslinging his stony trumpet, carried it, in his dying anguish, to his stony lips'. De Quincey explains these by association: the vision of the cathedral derived from a section of the road on which the mail-coach was travelling when the collision happened, where the trees met overhead in arches to suggest a vast nave; and the incident of the dying trumpeter was 'secretly suggested by my own imperfect effort to seize the guard's horn and to blow a warning blast'.

The three parts of 'The English Mail-Coach' make an extended, subtle, elaborate 'spot of time' or 'involute'. The whole is 'organic – i.e. . . . each acts upon all, and all react upon each', and its art is in the connections of the several parts. To catch and make real for us the shades and shapes, the hints and 'hieroglyphic suggestion' of dreams, De Quincey fashioned a fluid prose that was accurate but, of necessity, not precise; a prose of 'atmosphere' (his word) that could mould and communicate with power his own 'gleams of original feeling, [his] startling suggestions of novel thought'.

Appendix A

Masson, III, 462–3.

My second child, but eldest daughter, little M——, is between two and three weeks less than two years old: and from the day of her birth she has been uniformly attended by Barbara Lewthwaite. We are now in the first days of June; but, about three weeks since, consequently in the earlier half of May, some one of our neighbours gave to M—— a little bird. I am no great ornithologist. 'Perhaps only a tenth-rate one,' says some too flattering reader. Oh dear, no, nothing near it: I fear, no more than a 510th rater. Consequently, I cannot ornithologically describe or classify the bird. But I believe that it belonged to the family of finches – either a goldfinch, bull-finch, or at least something ending in *inch*. The present was less spendid than at first it seemed. For the bird was wounded, though not in a way that made the wound apparent; and too sensibly as the evening wore away it dropped. None of us knew what medical treatment to suggest; and all that occurred was to place it with free access to bird-seed and water. At length sunset arrived, which was the signal for M——'s depar-ture to bed. She came therefore as usual to me, threw her arms round my neck, and went through her ordinary routine of prayers: viz., the Lord's Prayer, and finally the four following lines (a Roman Catholic bequest to the children of Northern England):

> 'Holy Jesus, meek and mild,
> Look on me, a little child:
> Pity my simplicity;
> Grant that I may come to thee.'

M——, as she was moving off to bed, whispered to me that I was to 'mend' the bird with 'yoddonum'. Having always seen *me* taking laudanum, and for the purpose (as she was told) of growing better in health, reasonably it struck her that the little bird would improve under the same regimen. For her satisfaction, I placed a little diluted laudanum near to the bird; and she then departed to bed, though with uneasy looks reverting to her sick little pet. Occupied with some point of study, it happened that I sat up through the whole night: and long before seven o'clock in the morning she had summoned Barbara to dress her, and soon I heard the impatient little foot descending the stairs to my study. I had such a Jesuitical *bulletin* ready, by way of a report upon the bird's health, as might not seem absolutely despairing, though not too dangerously sanguine. And, as the morning was one of heavenly splendour, I proposed that we should improve the bird's chances by taking it out-of-doors into the little orchard at the foot of Fairfield – our loftiest Grasmere mountain. Thither moved at once Barbara Lewthwaite, little M——, myself, and the poor languishing bird. By that time in May, in any far southern county, perhaps the birds would be ceasing to sing; but not so with us dilatory people in Westmoreland. Suddenly, as we all stood around the little perch on which the bird rested, one thrilling song, louder than the rest, arose from a neighbouring hedge. Immediately the bird's eye, previously dull, kindled into momentary fire; the bird rose on its perch, struggled for an instant, seemed to be expanding its wings, made one aspiring movement upwards, in doing so fell back, and in another moment was dead. Too certainly and apparently all these transitions symbolically interpreted themselves, and to all of us alike: the proof of which was that man, woman, and child spontaneously shed tears: a weakness, perhaps, but more natural under the regular processional evolution of the scenical stages than when simply read as a narrative: for too evident it was, to one and all of us, without needing to communicate by words, *what* vision had revealed itself to all alike – to the child under two years old, not less than to the adults: too evident it was that, on this magnificent May morning, there had been exhibited, as on the stage of a theatre – there had passed before the eyes of us all – passed, and was finished

– the everlasting mystery of death! It seemed to me that little M——, by her sudden burst of tears, must have read this saddest of truths – must have felt that the bird's fate was sealed – not less clearly than Barbara or myself.

Appendix B

The Prelude (1805) Book XI, 258–328.

There are in our existence spots of time,
Which with distinct pre-eminence retain
260 A vivifying Virtue, whence, depress'd
By false opinion and contentious thought,
Or aught of heavier or more deadly weight,
In trivial occupations, and the round
Of ordinary intercourse, our minds
265 Are nourished and invisibly repair'd,
A virtue, by which pleasure is enhanced,
That penetrates, enables us to mount,
When high, more high, and lifts us up when fallen.
This efficacious spirit chiefly lurks
270 Among those passages of life in which
We have had deepest feeling that the mind
Is lord and master, and that outward sense
Is but the obedient servant of her will.
Such moments worthy of all gratitude,
275 Are scatter'd everywhere, taking their date
From our first childhood: in our childhood even
Perhaps are most conspicuous. Life with me,
As far as memory can look back, is full
Of this beneficent influence. At a time
280 When scarcely (I was then not six years old)
My hand could hold a bridle, with proud hopes
I mounted, and we rode towards the hills:
We were a pair of horsemen; honest James
Was with me, my encourager and guide.
285 We had not travell'd long, ere some mischance

Disjoin'd me from my Comrade, and, through fear
Dismounting, down the rough and stony Moor
I led my Horse, and stumbling on, at length
Came to a bottom, where in former times
290   A Murderer had been hung in iron chains.
The Gibbet-mast was moulder'd down, the bones
And iron case were gone; but on the turf,
Hard by, soon after that fell deed was wrought,
Some unknown hand had carved the Murderer's name.
295   The monumental writing was engraven
In times long past, and still, from year to year,
By superstition of the neighbourhood,
The grass is clear'd away; and to this hour
The letters are all fresh and visible.
300   Faltering, and ignorant where I was, at length
I chanced to espy those characters inscribed
On the green sod: forthwith I left the spot
And, reascending the bare Common, saw
A naked Pool that lay beneath the hills,
305   The Beacon on the summit, and more near,
A Girl who bore a Pitcher on her head
And seem'd with difficult steps to force her way
Against the blowing wind. It was, in truth,
An ordinary sight; but I should need
310   Colours and words that are unknown to man
To paint the visionary dreariness
Which, while I look'd all round for my lost guide,
Did at that time invest the naked Pool,
The Beacon on the lonely Eminence,
315   The Woman, and her garments vex'd and toss'd
By the strong wind. When, in a blessed season
With those two dear Ones, to my heart so dear,
When in the blessed time of early love,
Long afterwards, I roam'd about
320   In daily presence of this very scene,
Upon the naked pool and dreary crags,
And on the Melancholy Beacon, fell
The spirit of pleasure and youth's golden gleam;
And think ye not with radiance more divine

325   From these remembrances, and from the power
      They left behind? So feeling comes in aid
      Of feeling, and diversity of strength
      Attends us, if but once we have been strong.

Notes and References

Chapter 1: De Quincey and the Magazines

1. A. H. Japp, *Thomas De Quincey* (Edinburgh, 1890) pp. 75–6.
2. H. A. Eaton, *Thomas De Quincey* (London, 1936) p. 256.
3. Ibid.
4. Masson, I, 7.
5. De Quincey's money crises were very real, but were sometimes more real than at others; and his inexperience in money matters made him sometimes think that ready money was quite unready. See David Masson, *De Quincey* (London, 1909) pp. 104–5.
6. *The Rambler*, no. 184.
7. Masson, V, 233–4.
8. Ibid. I, 10, 12, 13.
9. Ibid. II, 139.
10. *Biographia Literaria*, ch. 1.
11. Masson, VII, 5–6.
12. René Wellek, *A History of Modern Criticism* (New Haven, 1965) III, 120.
13. Masson, II, 138.

Chapter 2: De Quincey and Wordsworth – I

1. John E. Jordan, *De Quincey to Wordsworth* (Berkeley and Los Angeles, 1962) pp. 36–7.
2. Masson, III, 302.
3. Ibid. III, 5, 61.
4. Ibid. III, 42.
5. Ibid.
6. Jordan, op. cit. pp. 31–2.
7. Ernest de Selincourt (ed.), *The Letters of William and Dorothy Wordsworth: The Early Years 1787–1805*, 2nd edn., revised C. L. Shaver (Oxford, 1967) p. 400.
8. Ibid. p. 454.
9. Jordan, op. cit. p. 39.
10. For De Quincey's account of the estrangement, see Masson, III, 197–206 and XI, 295–6.
11. Masson, I, 193.
12. Ibid., VII, 351.
13. Wordsworth was not impressed by her and did not share De Quincey's

squeamish response to other eighteenth-century novelists. See Masson,
III, 206.

14. Masson, XIV, 131.
15. Ibid. XI, 227–8.
16. George Eliot, *The Mill on the Floss*, Book VII, ch. 2.
17. Virginia Woolf, *The Common Reader* (second series), (London, 1932) pp. 137–8.
18. Masson, III, 209.
19. A. H. Japp (ed.), *The Posthumous Works of Thomas De Quincey* (London, 1893) pp. 209–10.
20. John E. Jordan, 'De Quincey on Wordsworth's Theory of Diction', *Publications of the Modern Languages Association of America* (1953) vol. LXVIII, pp. 764–78.
21. *Biographia Literaria*, ch. 4.
22. Masson, IX, 43.
23. Ibid. X, 342–59.

Chapter 3: De Quincey and Wordsworth – II

1. John E. Jordan, *De Quincey to Wordsworth*, p. 357.
2. Masson, II, 268.
3. Jordan, op. cit. pp. 1, 7.
4. W. J. B. Owen and Jane Worthington Smyser (eds), *The Prose Works of William Wordsworth*, 3 vols. (Oxford, 1974) vol. II, p. 59.
5. Masson, XI, 315–22.
6. Ernest de Selincourt (ed.), *The Letters of William and Dorothy Wordsworth: The Middle Years 1806–1820*, 2nd edn, revised Mary Moorman and A. G. Hill, 2 vols. (Oxford 1969–70) vol. I, p. 268.
7. James Hogg, *De Quincey and his Friends* (London, 1895) pp. 92–3.
8. Masson, XI, 304–8.
9. Owen and Smyser, *Prose Works*, II, 78.
10. A. H. Japp, *Posthumous Works*, I, 227.
11. Masson, II, 73.
12. H. A. Eaton (ed.), *A Diary of Thomas De Quincey* (London, n.d.) p. 169.
13. Ernest de Selincourt (ed.), *The Letters of William and Dorothy Wordsworth: The Later Years 1821–1850*, 3 vols. (Oxford, 1939) vol. I, p. 275.
14. Masson, I, 131–2.
15. Ibid. XI, 88–9.
16. Ibid. XI, 321.
17. Ibid. II, 440–3.
18. See especially, Herbert Lindenberger, *On Wordsworth's 'Prelude'* (Princeton, 1963) pp. 9–15.
19. *The Borderers*, ll. 1468–9.
20. Masson, XIII, 300–18.

Chapter 4: Power and Knowledge

1. Masson, X, 48 n.
2. Owen and Smyser, *Prose Works*, III, 81.
3. Ibid. III, 82.

4. Helen Darbishire (ed.), *De Quincey's Literary Criticism* (London, 1909) p. 31.
5. *Biographia Literaria*, ch. 13.
6. Masson, IV, 288–320, XI, 51–95.
7. Ibid. IV, 308–9.
8. Ibid. XI, 90–2.
9. Jupp, *Posthumous Works*, II, pp. 189–90.
10. Masson, X, 134–245.
11. Ibid. V, 91.
12. Donald Davie, 'Personification', *Essays in Criticism*, XXXI, no. 2, pp. 91–104.
13. Masson, X, 91.
14. Jupp, *Postumous Works*, II, 190–1.
15. Ernest de Selincourt (ed.), *The Letters of William and Dorothy Wordsworth: The Middle Years 1806–1820*, vol. II, p. 301.
16. Masson, X, 125.

Chapter 5: The Art of Prose

1. Masson, I, 9–15.
2. Ibid. II, 346; III, 51; X, 230.
3. Ibid. I, 49.
4. Ibid.
5. Ibid. X, 270–2.
6. Ibid. II, 65.
7. Ibid. V, 91; III, 51; XI, 17.
8. Ibid. II, 346; XI, 36; XI, 21.
9. Ibid. III, 413; Jupp, *Posthumous Works*, II, 134–5.
10. *Biographia Literaria*, ch. 1.
11. Masson, XI, 469.
12. Ibid. III, 431.
13. Ibid. VI, 100.
14. Ibid. VI, 101–2.
15. Ibid. III, 266.
16. Ibid. X, 258–9.
17. Ibid. V, 234; X, 108; X, 105.
18. Stuart M. Tave (ed.), *New Essays by De Quincey* (Princeton, 1966) pp. 202–3.
19. Masson, X, 109 n.; 102.
20. Ibid. XI, 36.
21. Ibid. XI, 37.
22. Ibid. V, 204.
23. Ibid. II, 328–9.
24. Hogg, *De Quincey and his Friends*, pp. 53–4.
25. Jupp, *Posthumous Works*, II. 108.
26. Tave, *New Essays by De Quincey*, 203, 193; Masson, III, 83.
27. Masson, XIII, 270–330.
28. Ibid. XIII, 270 n.

Index

Addison, Joseph, 5–6, 107, 108
Aeschylus, 84
Arnold, Matthew, 54, 93
Augustine, St., 102
Austen, Jane, 26

Bacon, Francis, 95–6, 98, 113, 114
Barrow, Isaac, 111
Bronte, Emily, 26
Brown, Sir Thomas, 95, 97, 99,
    100, 110, 111, 112
Burke, Edmund, 7–8, 46, 97, 99,
    110, 112–13
Burton, Robert, 113

Chaucer, Geoffrey, 18, 84
Chesterfield, Earl of, 8
Chillingworth, William, 111
Coleridge, Samuel Taylor, 11–12,
    13, 17, 18, 19, 21, 23, 24, 34,
    37, 38, 40, 46, 50, 57, 65, 78,
    81, 94, 109, 115, 117
Crabbe, George, 53, 54

Darbishire, Helen, 78
Davie, Donald, 94
De Quincey, Thomas
    Autobiography, 62, 65, 66, 68, 72,
        104
    Confessions, 2, 10–11, 12, 16, 24,
        36, 37, 49, 64, 67, 68, 69, 70,
        71, 102
    'English Mail-Coach, The', 12,
        74–5, 118–21
    'Last Days of Emmanuel Kant,
        The', 11
    Letters to a Young Man, 80–1
    'Life of Pope', 85
    'Lord Carlisle on Pope', 85
    'Oliver Goldsmith', 82

'On the Knocking at the Gate in
    Macbeth', 12, 13, 48
'Poetry of Pope, The', 82, 85
'Rhetoric', 94–100
'Ricardo', 110
'Style', 89–92
Suspiria de Profundis, 12, 54, 57,
    69, 70, 71, 102, 118
'Theory of Greek Tragedy', 43
'Wordsworth's Poetry', 38
Defoe, Daniel, 27, 107
Demosthenes, 110, 111
Dickens, Charles, 26, 28
Donne, John, 97, 99, 111
Dryden, John, 18, 84, 85

Eliot, George, 35
Euripides, 43–4

Fielding, Henry, 26, 30
Forster, E. M., 29
Fox, Charles James, 108, 114

Goethe, 32, 34
Goldsmith, Oliver, 28

Hazlitt, William, 116–17
Herodotus, 110–11
Hogg's Edinburgh Weekly Instructor, 3
Homer, 67, 111
    Iliad, 33, 67
    Odyssey, 67
Hood, Thomas, 115
Horace, 87

Inchbald, Elizabeth, 32, 33
Isocrates, 111

Japp, A. H., 38
Jeffrey, Francis, 54

131

Junius, 111

Kant, Emmanuel, 1, 11, 37, 81
Keats, John, 48

Lamb, Charles, 82, 116, 117–18
Locke, John, 35
Lockhart, J. G., 3
London Magazine, 1, 2, 13, 24, 25, 69, 80

Masson, David, 95
Milton, John, 20, 48, 60, 70, 111
 Paradise Lost, 81, 83–4, 86–7
 Paradise Regained, 99

Newton, Isaac, 84
North British Review, 3

Plato, 1, 93
Pope, Alexander, 18, 82–3, 84–6
 Dunciad, The, 85–6
 Essay on Criticism, 85, 87–8, 113
 Essay on Man, An, 85
 Imitations of Horace, 85
 Moral Epistles, 85
 Rape of the Lock, The, 85

Quarterly Review, 3

Radcliffe, Ann, 30, 31
Raleigh, Sir Walter, 98
Reynolds, Sir Joshua, 27
Ricardo, David, 11
Richardson, Samuel, 30
Rousseau, J. J., 36, 102

Scott, Sir Walter, 26, 27, 29
Shakespeare, William, 39–40, 85, 95, 100
 Hamlet, 84
 King Lear, 81, 84
 Macbeth, 84
 Othello, 84
Shelley, Percy Bysshe, 48, 51
Smollett, Tobias, 30
South, Robert, 111
Southey, Robert, 18, 38, 102, 108, 115

Spinoza, 11
Swift, Jonathan, 107, 108

Tait's Magazine, 3, 63
Taylor, Jeremy, 95, 97, 99, 100, 110, 111, 112–13, 114

Virgil, 87

Wilson, John ('Christopher North'), 2, 16
Woolf, Virginia, 36
Wordsworth, William
 'Complaint of a Forsaken Indian Woman', 64
 Essay, Supplementary to the Preface (1815), 76, 78, 79, 80
 Essays Upon Epitaphs, 23, 37, 40, 44–7, 51, 55–61
 Excursion, The, 23, 39, 50
 'Hart-Leap Well', 58
 'Idiot Boy, The' 50
 'I wandered lonely as a cloud', 68
 'Laodamia', 39
 Lyrical Ballads, 11, 13, 15, 16, 17, 19, 20, 22, 23, 37, 49, 50, 51, 58, 61, 63, 64, 65, 86
 'Margaret', *see* 'Ruined Cottage, The'
 'Michael', 41–2, 50
 'Nutting', 59–60
 Peter Bell, 57
 'Preface to the Edition of 1815', 78, 80
 'Preface' to *Lyrical Ballads*, 23, 24, 28, 29, 37, 38, 39, 40, 44, 46, 60, 61, 95
 Recluse, The, 11, 21
 'Ruined Cottage, The', 54–5
 'Ruth', 16
 'Simon Lee', 44, 62, 64
 'Stepping Westward', 44
 'Strange Fits of Passion', 119
 'Two April Mornings, The', 65, 67, 72
 'We Are Seven', 15, 52, 58, 64–5